Personal Success in a Team Environment

It's Your LIfe and Career

Les Wallace, Ph.D.
Dennis Derr, Ed.D.
Eric Meade, MBA

Les Wallace, Ph.D.
President
Signature Resources Inc.
PO Box 460100
Aurora, CO 80046

Les@signatureresources.com

www.signatureresources.com

Personal Success

Library of Congress Cataloging-in-Publication Data

Les Wallace Ph.D. Dennis Derr Ed.D. Eric Meade MBA
Personal Success in a Team Environment
Includes bibliographical references
ISBN-13: 978-1499220087
ISBN-10: 1499220081

Contents

Introduction

Today's workplace is a complicated mix of performance expectations, collaboration and teamwork, technology, and internal or external customer demands. Then there's management who is feeling the pressure for their unit to perform. As a staff member, professional or someone entering management for the first time, you are probably facing challenges you didn't encounter even as recently as five years ago. You may even feel a level of stress and responsibility that you have not known before in your career. Sometimes it can all feel a bit overwhelming.

Fortunately, there are skills you can learn and apply that will help you maintain perspective and prevent the stress from becoming too much for you to handle. There are ways of thinking about your current role and responsibilities that can keep you on task and keep you performing at your best. It is important to keep in mind that **we work to live, we don't live to work.** And as this book will show you, the point is to live a good, healthy life, as you yourself define it.

Of course it is no wonder that many of us at times find ourselves struggling not to let workplace challenges drain the energy out of our personal lives. Nor is it a surprise that the normal challenges of personal life frequently hamper our wellbeing and our performance while we are at work. Our lives – the personal, the professional, and everything else – are complex social systems. That means that they are made up of many interrelated parts and seemingly little events can yield hugely significant consequences. Thus it takes a consistent openness to constant learning to discover how to live a successful and fulfilling life. Life is full of change–for all of us. Some people struggle to cope with the slightest hiccup. But others seem able to stay focused and happy even as the dust swirls around them, adapting to change and succeeding amidst uncertainty.

We wrote this book in the hope that we can offer you, the reader, some useful hints, tips, strategies, and skills that you can apply to your life and work so that you can create a life that is successful and fulfilling. We know something about the classic human behaviors that often get in the way of success as well as about the behaviors and commitments that successful people appear to have in common. That is what this self-study workbook is all about.

What we know about successful people is that they know where they want to go and they prepare to make the journey. They have a vision and a plan to make it a reality. There are many successful people who have been "lucky" and maybe you hope you too can be lucky. Well, let's set the record straight about luck: **luck is where preparation and opportunity come together.** Yes there is some blinding luck like winning the lottery. But luck in your life will most likely be a blend of clear expectations, hard work on your part and flexibility.

Our learning journey begins with two short chapters that explore common lessons for those seeking greater success in their lives, and common reasons why personal and professional setbacks happen. These articles set up several chapters of skill review and application and self-reflection on the common challenges of life and work, and on how to energize success as you define it.

Successful people are continuous learners. Through often difficult experiences, they develop new skills and build new strength so that they can take on future challenges. And then they encounter other difficult situations that require them to develop new skills and strength all over again. The cycle continues. Life, it seems, is a learning journey, and some of this learning is prompted by setbacks. The learning never stops, and the more you commit to it the more successful you will be–in all aspects of your life.

In that spirit, we offer you our best advice on personal success in a team environment.

Best wishes,

Les Wallace, Ph.D.
Dennis Derr, Ed.D.
Eric Meade, MBA

CHAPTER 1

Ten Important Lessons for Those Seeking Personal Success

"The sad news is, nobody owes you a career. Your career is literally your business. You own it as a sole proprietor. You have one employee: yourself. You are in competition with millions of similar businesses: millions of other employees all over the world. You need to accept ownership of your career, your skills and the timing of your moves."

Andrew Grove

Success is a choice. Every day your life will test you in some way and your responses to these tests will produce the results that will make up your life. The choice is yours--everyday the **"will" to grow, improve, and seek new levels of achievement helps set the successful apart from those who muddle along in misery and mediocrity.** No excuses. You're not a victim. Make a decision today to accelerate your success. What are you waiting for?

It's more about what YOU do than about how you're treated. To a great extent we create our own reality. While bad things happen to everyone, most of life's ups and downs are of our own creation based on our own perceptions of how we frame the experience. Look through history at the success stories of people and you'll find common elements: (a) they all had challenges, many of them serious; (b) they all set goals, learned, changed, and (c) made a choice to be persistent in finding opportunity based on (a) and (b). Pay attention to the attitude you bring to your life, and you will find opportunities even in your darkest hour.

Success in life and work is about relationships. Few of us go through life alone. Our human social networks, personal and at work, contribute to, or, challenge our success and wellbeing. Interpersonal competence can be learned and improved. While you don't have to like everybody with whom you come in contact, successful people do seem more adept at adapting to the diverse relationships necessary to be happy and achieve success.

Success is about continuous transformation. "Constant change" is readily recognized as the norm in human life; it is also the norm in organizational life. Try to be active rather than over reactive. Pay attention to trends and changes at work and seek advice on what they may mean for you. Successful people tend to be more flexible, alert to the choices facing them and actively seek to make change work for them.

Connect the Dots. Meaningful success is never all about you. There is old adage about two stonemasons in the Middle Ages who were asked what they were doing. One said, "I'm cutting this stone." The other said, "I'm building a cathedral." In a climate of success, people believe in the larger importance of their work and feel connected to an energizing vision of their life and work. A belief in "purpose" is well known to help people deal more confidently and successfully with the stress and challenge of transition and problem solving.

Focus on the Vital Few. Having an overly ambitious, busy set of priorities is a common mistake that hinders personal and professional success. Successful people have big dreams but they whittle down a long list of priorities and initiatives to a "vital few" which will return the most on their investment effort.

It is wise to follow the old 80/20 rule here, which states that **20% of your priorities will most likely give you 80% of the success you seek?** Focus on those 20%. Give up some, scale back energy on others and surround your key objectives with high energy and massive focus. The strategy is to think big while acting in small steps toward the goal.

Succeed by helping others succeed. Recent research suggests that efforts to develop others pay some of the highest return in terms of our own personal growth. Helping others is a "differentiating" behavior with a positive ripple effect on other key success behaviors such as goal achievement, interpersonal relationships, adaptability and communication. Not only do we grow in all these areas, but also our efforts to develop others contribute to our own confidence, personal credibility and continued learning.

Make it Happen. Detours, barriers, lack of cooperation, risk and sudden shifts in work and life derail the average person from forging ahead with their dreams. Many people seem to celebrate these barriers more than focusing on their own actions. But a barrier is just a dressed up excuse; the person citing the barrier sounds thoughtful and conscientious, but in fact they are simply letting themselves off the hook for not taking the actions required to reach their goals. Successful people stay focused and bring a realistic "can do" attitude to critical success objectives. This doesn't mean a Pollyanna view of challenges. It does mean that successful people never see themselves as victims and rarely take no for an answer. They are adept at being flexible and discovering pathways that get to goals despite challenging conditions.

Setbacks are a key to success. Most of life is recovering from mis-steps or the challenges provided by trying to live happy and healthy. Successful people understand this and don't take setback as failure. Most successful people don't refer to, or see, failure. Instead they recognize not all outcomes will be optimal and some may even be disastrous at first but they are only failures if we give up or fail to learn. **Getting up, dusting yourself off and re-engaging the challenge is what success is all about. Life may be a series of recoveries and so is**

personal success. Learn, adapt, change directions and go again. But fail? Not in our vocabulary.

Success means living with integrity. We could have started here because it all begins and ends with integrity. Many people think they have it, and in a general sense they are probably right. But the success we write about here is **beyond reproach**. Taking your life to higher personal and professional success can be done through lots of approaches, many of which lack integrity. Short-term selfishness, spikes in performance coming from hurting others or playing loose with the rules is not true success. Remember that once you give up integrity, it is extremely hard to get it back in the eyes of those around you.

"Since the mind is a specific biocomputer; it needs specific instructions and directions.

The reasons most people never reach their goals is that they don't define them, learn about them, or ever seriously consider them as believable or achievable.

Successful people can tell you where they are going, what they plan to do along the way, and who will be sharing the adventure with them."

Dennis Whatley

"To change one's life:
Start Immediately
Do it flamboyantly
No Exceptions"

William James

CHAPTER 2

Ten Common Reasons
for Personal and Professional Setback

*"The greatest discovery of my generation is that a
human being can alter their life by altering their attitude."*

William James

This chapter presents you with ten common reasons for the personal and professional setbacks that delay or prevent us from achieving our vision. How we respond to these setbacks may be the greatest determinant of our future success.

Poor interpersonal skills. Life and work are both social environments where communication, sensitivity and compromise are required for success. Getting along is more than simply putting up with difficult situations. Getting along requires active work to make interpersonal situations work for you. If portions of your interpersonal resume need strengthening seek out the many sources at work and in the community to grow your portfolio of skills. These will be yours for life!

What interpersonal skill do you know today that you need to work on?

Wrong fit. When it's clear you're in the wrong job or relationship the ball's in your court to seek a better situation. Trying to tough it out hoping it will get better may not be your best option. Remember that doing the same thing over and over that doesn't work while expecting different results may be a sign something is wrong. Hope is not a strategy. Get some career or personal advice, assess your choices, and make new plans.

What in your life may currently be a wrong fit and out of sync?

Half-hearted effort—Not fulfilling commitment. While we all have variations in our focus and follow-through, trying to squeak by knowing you're cutting corners will always catch up with you. Friends, co-workers and supervisors know who gives reasonable effort and future relationships will be impacted by your choices.

Everybody knows who the slackers are. What do co-workers think about you?

Bad Luck. Bad things happen to good people: car repairs when money's tight, a new boss with an abrasive style, a relationship that disintegrates, a chronic illness. Hardy people seek appropriate help, hunker down with focus and determination and consider the choices in their life to help recover.

What's your recovery style? Victim? (Blame it on someone or something else) Planner? (Build a plan to create a solution) Strong willed? (Power through no matter what).

Self-Destructive Behavior. Chronically grumpy, negative and contentious people never gain credibility. Poor personal habits deteriorate your health and relationships (boss, co-worker, friends); poor work habits keep the supervisor on your back; negativity makes you stand out like the proverbial sore thumb. Such behavior invites bad things into our life and is our own fault. If you are chronically this way you may need professional help.

Choose to walk away from the temptation to make bad choices. You know them!

Lack of Focus. Dreams and goals without plans rarely get accomplished. Where do you want to go? What are you willing to invest to get there? Then get going. Don't worry about how fast you move, just move!

What's your goal? Your plan? Talk with friends, experts, family and write it down. Put it where you can see it everyday. [See Chapter 10 for some career planning guidance.]

Discrimination. Stereotyping, bad blood, favoritism are all part of the human landscape both social and work. We all struggle with objectivity in dealing with people we don't know well or those for whom we carry a negative stereotype. If you get caught in an unfair situation at work, check your options with your human resource department. If you get caught in an unfair personal situation, check your options and make some changes.

Discrimination can happen to any of us. But, are we also guilty of discriminating?

Misuse of time. First things first. If we lived by that advice we would most likely be less stressed and more successful. The big question is do you have a good concept of what is first? People with focus (see # 6) seem to use their time more wisely because they know what they want, what to invest in to get it and what is a waste of effort. What changes should you make here?

Start small by cleaning up a few time wasters; go big by setting new goals.

Hanging on when you should move on. Most of us learned this lesson in school when we moved between friends and groups knowing when a change was in our best interest. You may be the strong one but that doesn't make hanging on to a bad situation the right choice. Check your options because you always have options.

Are you in a situation where you should move on?

Failing to learn. Whatever your current level of success, you should always be learning. A good learner—without changing events—can make the concept of failure disappear. Seek first to understand what is actually happening, then make genuine change based on what you've learned. And be honest with yourself: no matter what the situation, there's also some learning in there for us.

Recall some lessons you've learned from bad and good choices. Are you putting those lessons to good use?

"Life is a test. It is only a test. Had this been a real life you would have been instructed where to go and what to do."

"Remember that you become what you practice the most."

"Think of your problems as potential teachers."

Richard Carlson, <u>Don't Sweat the Small Stuff</u>

CHAPTER 3

"Unlocking the Puzzle of Personal Success"

"Ten years from now you will be more disappointed by the things you didn't do than by the ones you did. So throw off the bowlines. Sail away from the safe harbor. Catch the trade winds in your sails. Explore. Dream. Discover."

Mark Twain

Personal Success and Your Organization's Mission

You were hired to deliver something. Zeroing in on what it is and why its valuable may help you discover opportunities for greater success.

Considering your current job, who are your customers?
    Citizens?
    Purchasers / Users?
    Internal Customer?
    Your manager(s)?

What do your customers expect?
    As a staff member or front line manager how might you find out?

Why is your work valuable? How does it connect to or fulfill the end users and customer's needs?

> External Customer?
>
> Internal Customer?
>
> Your manager(s)?

Defining Success

Success: the achievement of something desired, planned, or attempted.

Defining Success: What elements of success are important to you? What does success look like for you? Personal happiness? Achievement at work?

Here are some responses from other people who reflected on what success looks like from our workshops:

- The ability to use my talents at work—doing what I do best to enhance my work environment.
- Good results, growth, happiness.
- Helping others be and do their best in their jobs and career.
- Achieving each goal I set—both big and small.
- 100% attendance.
- Satisfying someone's need. Making them smile.
- Involved, busy, succeeding at job assignments.
- Valued for contribution, opportunities for involvement, empowered, advancement in positions.
- Solving a problem.
- Due dates met, customer need met, a valued member of the team, meeting work expectations.
- Improving each day, never quit learning.
- Clean house, happy family, supper on the stove, dogs at my feet.
- Good home life, money to pay the bills, free time to enjoy life.

- Making the world a better place, within my space of influence.
- Being the best I can be.
- My children and grandchildren are happy, responsible, & successful.
- I can find peace in my everyday life.
- Enjoy what I am doing, feel recognized, feel valued.

What's common from these perspectives on success?

Here are some responses from others identifying challenges and barriers to success at work:

- High stakes work.
- Grumpy boss / co-workers.
- Family challenges.
- Not certain what's really important.
- What's important changes often.
- No one listens to my ideas
- New boss.
- Single parent—lots on my mind.
- Not good at communicating.
- Too much stress.
- Stuck in low end job.

What's common from these comments identifying challenges to success?

Personal Success in a Team Environment: Exercise

What's your personal motivation for wanting to be more successful?
For yourself personally?
With your family?
With your work?
With your immediate manager?
With your team?

Personal Success in a Team Environment

Based upon your reflection, what's needed for your success in a team environment?

- _____

- _____

- _____

- _____

- _____

- _____

Now, as you work through the remaining chapters note the content that may provide the most help in achieving success with these elements.

How Successful Do YOU Want to Be?

Self Assess Your Workplace Situation
A "1" rating means "Uncertain." A "5" rating means "Very Clear."

I know what's expected...
1. My organization's mission?
   1   2   3   4   5

2. My organization's vision?
   1   2   3   4   5

3. My organization's key performance goals?
   1   2   3   4   5

4. How my unit contributes and what specifically we need to deliver?
   1   2   3   4   5

5. How my individual performance on critical job elements impacts organizational success?
   1   2   3   4   5

6. What's changing, why, and how it will happen?
   1   2   3   4   5

Based on this assessment, where might you need greater clarity from your manager?

How Successful Do YOU Want to Be?

Self Assess Your Workplace Situation
A "1" rating means "Uncertain." A "5" rating means "Very Clear."

I'm fully engaged because I understand…
1. Why my engagement is important and what's in it for me?
   1   2   3   4   5

2. That my work outcomes, teamwork and customer focus are appreciated?
   1   2   3   4   5

3. How I can continue to grow and possibly advance in the organization?
   1   2   3   4   5

4. How my performance will be evaluated?
   1   2   3   4   5

5. When and how I will get feedback and coaching?
   1   2   3   4   5

6. How the resources of the organization can help me be successful?
   1   2   3   4   5

Based on this assessment:
Where do I need clarity from my manager?

Would a "performance check" discussion be beneficial?

How Successful Do YOU Want to Be?

Self Assess Your Workplace Situation
   A "1" rating means "Uncertain." A "5" rating means "Very Clear."

I can be successful because...
   1. I have the necessary skills and strengths to be successful?
      1   2   3   4   5

   2. I know what skills I need to develop?
      1   2   3   4   5

   3. I know how the organization can support my efforts?
      1   2   3   4   5

   4. I know how I can contribute ideas to improve our organizational success?
      1   2   3   4   5

   5. My manager cares about me being successful by providing development opportunities?
      1   2   3   4   5

Based on this assessment:
What assistance could you seek from your manager to be more successful?

On what "developmental" initiatives should you personally engage?

> **"Your ability to get another job will be directly related**
> **to how well you do on the job you have now."**

Look at Employee Engagement in Your Organization

Employee workplace engagement is demonstrated by behaviors indicating functional capability: the employee knows the job and can do it as required most of the time.

Workplace engagement is also demonstrated by behaviors indicating high commitment to the team, the organization and the employee's own role. That is, employees cooperate to solve problems, enhance teamwork, and offer ideas to improve work and the organization.

We can vary in our ability or commitments to fully engage our workplace responsibilities. Take a look at these three levels of "employee engagement" and try to honestly assess your own engagement. **Where are you? How might you enhance your engagement and, therefore, your value to the organization?**

I. Instructive Phase Engagement:

An employee at this level of engagement has difficulty and is inconsistent with functional performance such as meeting task expectations, consistently good work habits and workplace behaviors. These employees continued to need instruction and closer oversight to perform.

> *What might cause this level of performance?*

> *What might an employee at this level of performance expect from their manager?*

If this is you, what choices or actions might you take to be more successful?

II. Interactive Phase Engagement:

An employee at this level of engagement demonstrates "functional capability" (doing the job satisfactorily and behaving according to organizational expectations). These employees are "interacting" with the workplace and team in a productive way.

What's required to stay functionally capable in our work?

What might an employee at this level of performance expect from their manager?

If this is you, what choices or actions might you take to be more successful?

III. Consultative Phase Engagement:

An employee at this level of engagement consistently achieves high levels of performance and teamwork. This employee excels in both task and interpersonal capabilities and frequently acts as peer consultant to team members and management.

What's required to achieve at this high level?

What might we expect from management at this level of performance?

If this is you, what's required to remain at this level?

On the next couple of pages let's look more closely at specific behaviors that indicate a level of engagement. Look to find yourself in these descriptions—be honest in your assessment.

Please note: as we become successful at one level of work and get an opportunity to advance or be promoted, we are likely to cycle back through an "instructive" phase of learning until we get acclimated to the new work.

ASSESSMENT OF ENGAGEMENT

Typical Employee Behaviors in Instructive Phase Engagement:	**Typical Employee Behavior in Interactive Phase Engagement**
Criticizes without suggestions.	May criticize but offers suggestions.
Inconsistent productivity.	Consistent productivity
Unable to evaluate his/her own performance.	Capable of identifying improvement needs; seeks assistance.
Frequently waits to be told what to do next.	Seeks out meaningful tasks to fill voids; assists others.
Doesn't assist others without being told.	Assists others without being asked.
Always asks before taking action-- reluctant to take independent responsibility.	Frequently accepts independent responsibility.
Tense and uncomfortable with adversity and stress.	Able to identify causes of stress and manage most work challenges.
Uncertain of the decision making process.	Understands and participates in decision making processes.
Shows little interest in the "rationale" behind decisions and tasks.	Inquires about decisions and tasks to better understand work and decision making processes.

Inconsistent acceptable conduct.	Conduct consistently acceptable.
Unable to understand customer need and points of view.	Understands customer needs and provides quality service.
Cooperates with team members when told to do so.	Willingly seeks to work cooperatively with team members.

If your behaviors look like these, what might you do to move from this Instructive Phase?

What's the difference between these two lists?

ASSESSMENT OF ENGAGEMENT

Typical Employee Behaviors in Interactive Phase Engagement	Typical Employee Behaviors in Consultative Phase Engagement
May criticize but offers suggestions.	Suggestions thought out for impact on work, customers & co-workers.
Consistent productivity.	Consistently exceeds expectations.
Capable of identifying improvement needs; seeks assistance.	Self assesses improvement needs and develops plan; seeks training and learning.
Fills voids with meaningful tasks.	Anticipates workflow & stays busy.

Assists others without being asked.	Acts as a source of information and assistance to others.
Frequently accepts independent responsibility.	Comfortable taking independent responsibility for decisions
Able to identify causes of stress and manages most effectively.	Maintains even disposition; assists others with stressful events.
Understands and participates in decision making process.	Actively participates in and helps lead decision making processes.
Inquires about "rationale" behind decisions and tasks to better understand decision making processes and work.	Relates "rationale" for decisions and tasks to overall goals and objectives.
Conduct consistently acceptable.	Exemplary conduct / role model.
Understands customer needs and provides quality services.	Delivers exceptional service and acts as "voice" of the customer.
Willingly seeks to work cooperatively with team members.	Models collaboration, supports team members, and facilitates teamness.

If your behaviors look like these, what might you
Do to move to the consultative phase.

What's the difference between these two lists?

Reflecting on your engagement

At what level of engagement do you believe others see you?

How might you check your perception?

At what level of engagement do you believe your manager sees you?

How might you find out?

What might you do to assure you're recognized at the consultative level of engagement?

Who might be a helpful coach or mentor to improving your level of engagement?

Review and Key Points

"Success will not lower its standard to us.
We must raise our standard to success."

Rev. Randall R. McBride, Jr.

- **To be successful you must clearly understand the expectations of your work.**

   Do you need a clarity check on anything? Don't wait, seek clarity.

- **To be successful you must understand how you can continue to grow and develop and possibly advance within the organization.**

   What's your development plan?

   How can your manager help here? Have you asked for help?

   Who else can help you? Have you asked for help?

   What can you do without asking for permission (read, workshops, get a mentor)?

- **What do you believe your current level of engagement to be?**

   Instructive?

   Interactive?

   Consultative?

Do you know how others see your engagement?

Do you know how your manager sees your engagement?

What might you work on to improve or sustain your level of engagement?

"You don't just stumble into the future. You create your own future."

Visualizing Success

Earlier in this chapter, we defined success as "the achievement of something desired, planned, or attempted." That means that success is impossible if you have not yet articulated the desires you have for your own future. If you are simply "fire-fighting" – that is, reacting to daily crises with little sense of where you are headed over the long term – then you are unlikely to be successful, even if you are highly effective at "fighting fires."

For most of us, our desires reach out further in time than the situations we have before us today. Perhaps we want to become a senior manager within our company. Perhaps we want to build a healthy family. Perhaps we want to learn a set of skills so that we can set up our own company. These aspirations are long-term; they demand consistent effort over a period of several years at least. Stating one's aspirations is important, but we invite you to go even further. Try to embody the future you want to create for yourself.

First, state in very specific terms what you would like to create for yourself. Make sure that you really spell it out. If it's a professional aspiration, then where will you work, what will your job be, with whom will you be spending your time, etc.? If the aspiration is related to your home and family, then where will you live, what will be happening in the lives of your loved ones, how will you interact with them, etc.?

Now sit back and imagine that you have achieved that aspiration. Visualize that you have been successful. What does it feel like? What emotions come up for you when you envision yourself in that future? How might you carry yourself physically once you have achieved that future? You might even walk around as you imagine your success and just see what it feels like.

Once you have imagined what it will feel like to be successful, you will likely feel an even greater commitment to the aspirations you have stated. It may feel so great that you don't want to wait any longer than you have to. We invite you to start feeling that way now. Start carrying yourself today the same way you will carry yourself once you have achieved your goals. You have heard that "success breeds success." So internalize the success you want – even if it is only in your imagination – and let that feeling of success become a reality in your life.

Of course, it may be that imagining your success raises strong feelings in you of self-doubt. Self-doubt is a perfectly appropriate emotion when you are trying something you have never done before. But if you find that the feelings of self-doubt are sabotaging your efforts or undermining your motivation, then talk to your manager, friends, family, or perhaps a professional coach to identify and break through the assumptions you have about yourself that may be limiting your success.

CHAPTER 4

Use of Time and Considerations for Success

Balance vs. Navigation

Much talk has occurred in the 21st Century about the need for balance in our lives--the stated need to balance work, family and self and to proportion time accordingly. Whatever you feel balance is, it's not going to happen unless you get intentional about it. We might be better off to think of our work-life-personal journey as just that—a journey. A journey that you can navigate with shifting balance when necessary, e.g. more family time when it's called for and more work focus when it accelerates your success goals without abandoning what's important to you.

Navigators have clear destinations but realize changing course may also be necessary. Not much goes in a straight line today, certainly not our lives. So, successful people think consciously about their time investments and they select their choices and emotions like they select their clothes—everyday for a specific journey.

Time in an Era of 24 hours a day / 7 days a week: E + R = QT

If we had a nickel for every time someone tried to waste our time, we'd be wealthy. If we had a nickel for every time we wasted our own time, we'd be even wealthier. If we had a penny for every time a client whined about not enough time, well, you get it. And it seems to be getting worse. Many parents are so busy they've taken to referring to their children as tasks 4 and 5.

You know the drill: it started with facsimile machines when people seemed to back off timely work deadlines because they could fax at the last minute. It migrated to cellular phones when customers and our managers felt they could reach us anytime and anywhere time and space came together. It accelerated with the Internet when Mable two cubicles down would email you at 8:45am about a 9am meeting, assuming of course that you stare at your device awaiting the ping of every email. And it seems to be getting worse. Can you say Instant Messaging?

Please take a vow to use time, yours and others, wisely. To be quick when it's in your mutual interest and to reflect when it's also in your mutual interest. E for efficiency and R for reflection. The E part will stress you and the R part will nourish you. If you get the right combinations working in your work and life you will have achieved a *quality time* (QT) approach to spending your days that will lead to greater sanity and longer life

Efficiency. Simple can frequently do when complex looks more powerful. Discover the difference. In your communication, your work plans, your life. What might you be able to simplify right now?

Efficiency. Being ready to make the most of the professional work and life chores. Take something to read (work or pleasure) when you know there is likely to be a wait (doctor's office, airplane, car pool home from soccer practice).

Recognize that roughly right more likely than not beats precisely perfect.

Teach others how to bring you information, ideas, requests in an efficient manner to cut both time and frustration from your life.

Cluster like chores and slam dunk them for both efficiency and mental health. Hustle when you can and it isn't unsafe so that you have more minutes for reflection.

Because we work to live; we don't live to work, efficiency with our work gives us more reflection in our lives which provides us *quality time* (QT).

Edge: assertiveness, discipline, ignoring the trivial

Successful people have "edge:" they are strong willed, resilient and make the tough decisions that less successful people won't make. They realize that no one will give them more time in their day or life and resolve to use the available time most wisely on what matters to them, their families, and their profession. Their secrets are no mystery. Summarized below are ten of the most common.

Where are You Going? In the next ninety days, the next six months / year, the next five years: what are your plans? Dreams? Professional goals and plans to get there? Goals without plans are rarely achieved. Successful people cannot only tell you where they are going but how they intend to get there. And, whether it's written out in a formal plan or scribbled on the back of an envelope—it is written out. Steven Covey called this our "compass." And without a compass, the clock simply ticks without purpose and urgency frequently smothers importance.

Stop Doing List. Once a quarter look at your plate...your entire plate: professional, family, social. What must you stop doing so that you can free more time for what matters. Successful people use this discipline. And finding adequate time for reflection/recharging is a worthy reason to stop doing something less important. Look to free up one hour a week personal and one hour a week business as a good starting point.

Yes's Count by Saying NO! Make your "yes's" more valuable by saying no to the less important. If you have clear priorities this is easy. Bosses, associates, community, friends will all try to get some of your time. Successful people are strong and say no to the trivial so that the important get enough oxygen.

90 Seconds. That's all you have to get my attention and permission to take more of my time. Get to the point: identify the issue, what you need from me, solution / plan outline. Don't come to me empty handed. If you need coaching, set up a separate coaching session so that I reserve time for us to get in deep. I expect you to do your homework before you get on my calendar. What's your elevator message? That's about how much time you have to convince me to give you more or send you packing. If you can hook me I'll invest more time. Now, teach those who approach you to use this concise motif also. You're smart enough to know when to say "Whoa, we need to set an appointment to sit down and talk this through more thoroughly."

Powerful Meetings. Meetings encroach upon thirty to seventy percent of a busy person's professional life and are potentially serious time wasters. Let the sun set on all regularly scheduled meetings and then reinstitute sessions based upon the next three months priorities. Excuse yourself from ones where your hand is not needed; hold quick 20 minute stand-up meetings for many topics / problems [they really become more efficient]; demand an agenda for each and every meeting or don't go. Clarify the desired outcome of each meeting at the outset and stay focused on delivering it. Maybe someone else can benefit by sitting in for you while you benefit by investing in your compass.

Ruthlessly Sort and Delete Email. The email disease grips less successful people. They blame the technology or others for the time they spend on email but really have only themselves to blame. This valuable communication device is handled with amateur capability by most. Most systems now have automatic files into which you can flow sources and topics of email to assure priority sorting and not missing something significant. Most of us can look at the list of emails and tell by source or subject line which to bother with and which we can safely overlook. Many of us can use only the subject line for up to 50% of our correspondence: give a decision, ask for information, say thanks, etc. All of us can create community email guidelines agreed upon by our close contact team to save time and assure value. You are not likely to miss something significant on email: the critical and emergency stuff will find you in other ways. Turn off your device's "incoming mail ping." Check email only 4-5 times each day and please, please, only use "reply to all" once in 1,000 times.

Ban PowerPoint™ or Severely Limit its Use. This pandemic use of a simple visual aid has added hours of unnecessary gibberish and nonsense to presentations and turned simple communication into death by PowerPoint™. Teach and expect people around you to communicate clearly and succinctly and spare us the technological vaporization of valuable time in production and presentation. [See our essay "Ten Guidelines if You Really Must Use PowerPoint." Signatureresources.com]

Personal Contracts. We make commitments and we dodge commitments. When commitments are important for your sanity, let's say to your family or children, make a contract. Children as little as 3 years can understand a contract posted on the fridge: "Dad will be home early on Tuesday to go to the park." "Trinity will put her toys away every evening at 7pm." The more stressful it is for you to erode a commitment (like to your children or spouse) the more important it is to make a contract. This binds our commitments and makes it easier for us to manage time to fulfill our contract. Someone at work repeatedly wastes your time: make a contract with full expectations for both of you. It works, try it!

People and Relationships vs Schedules and Things. So how do effective leaders skinny down their time commitments but bolster their investment in people? Effective leaders strategically plan their contacts to assure communication gets diffused, appreciation doesn't slip, and developing others remains a primary commitment. Remember the earlier "where are you going" question? Well, those who have a clear focus and compass manage to find plenty of time to build relationships. That visit to the going away retirement party may not be wasted time if you go with networking purpose. Dropping in on the monthly birthday reception is not a waste if you use the contact wisely. There is no such thing as casual schmoozing—make it purposeful.

Uninterrupted Time Each Day / Year. Every single time management treatise suggests this. Usually in the morning if you can. Keep that calendar clear. If there's an emergency someone will find you. If not, you can clear your head and maintain your priority focus. Give yourself permission to think. And those vacations you put off--successful people find time for themselves and don't end up the year with "use or lose" vacation time. Few of us are so important we can't get away for a few days every now and then.

Polls of U.S. workers find that about 30% of us regularly fail to use all our allotted vacation days.

Increasing Personal Success through Priority Management

*"Anything less than a conscious commitment to the important
is an unconscious commitment to the unimportant."*

Steven Covey

Take a look at this matrix created by Steven Covey to help people determine in which quadrant of activities you spend your workday. I and II are where success lives. III and IV can grow on the undisciplined person and erode time spent on success producing activities.

I. Urgent & Important	II. Not Urgent Yet Important
■ Work & projects critical to your position description. ■ Solving quality and timeliness challenges. ■ Work schedules. ■ Full cooperation with team. ■ Work crises response & support.	■ Clarification of changing situation. ■ Planning for the future. ■ Relationship building. ■ Personal Development and Learning. ■ Participation in team problem solving.
"Here is where we focus and bring our experience to bear on critical challenges and opportunities."	*"This quadrant doesn't act upon us, we must act upon it. Action here prevents many things from becoming urgent."*

III. Urgent Attention Yet Not Important	IV. Not Urgent & Not Important
■ Interruptions, some phone calls. ■ Some email. ■ Many popular activities; gossiping, complaining. *"The noise of urgency creates the illusion of importance."*	■ Trivia, busywork. ■ Junk mail. ■ Some phone calls. ■ Petty disagreements. ■ Excessive "stewing" vs letting go. ■ Personal time wasters. *"This is the quadrant of waste. It's deterioration, not survival."*

Adapted from: Steven Covey, © **First Things First** (1994)

"The art of being wise is the art of knowing what to overlook."
William James

Common Time Robbers

Research on successful people finds that they don't outperform the average person by leaps and bounds in time management. Successful people do find those few percentage points of discipline that allows them to gain an advantage.

The research on time management finds a few common ways in which the less successful let themselves be robbed of time. Peruse this list and see if you can find something you're doing that can be brought back into control of your time.

Working Without a Plan.

- Without priorities everything you do has equal importance: 20% of your actions produce 80% of your outcomes: does your plan focus on that 20%?
- **Become effective (focusing on "high payoff" items) before becoming efficient.**
- Set quarterly plans for work and monthly plans for home!

Action Item: Post priorities above your phone/computer, or on the fridge to stay vigilant.

Action Item: Create a "stop doing" list and clean up the 10% of what you're doing that you know wastes time. This will make your yes's more valuable.

Dishonest Priorities.

- Choosing to do the easiest or most fun activity first.
- Letting someone badger you into their activity instead of sticking to your priorities.
- Reading your email as if it was all a priority—hit delete fast and often!

Action Item: Always work from a "to do" list with success priorities first!

Action Item: Read email in priority order by source and your key objectives!

Unclear Responsibilities.

- Uncertain of priorities and how to manage time.
- Uncertain of "results" expected so work lacks focus.
- Poor attention to planning and clarifying assignments.

Action Item: Use this formula to clarify priorities with your manager: outcomes expected + rationale for priority + time line + available resources = clear assignment!

Action Item: Always stay clear with your manager on work priorities. Ask!

Procrastination.

- Break big projects into smaller segments to create cycles of immediate accomplishment.

Action Item: Batch like items and go on a "10 minute clearing frenzy."

Action Item: Give yourself a small reward for taking on something you've put off.

Communication Skills.

- Poor listening habits fail to clarify & understand priorities and perspective.
- Keep a notebook on staff meetings; keep a phone notebook/log.
- Keep meetings strictly on target; yours and others, including conference calls.
- Separate meeting topics from relationship topics. Mixing both creates long meetings. Shorter meetings will be weil received by all

Action Item: Pay attention. Paraphrase to assure meaning? Share lots of info.

Social Chit Chat and Interruptions

- Close off friendly conversations politely; move on.
- Let people know you only have a minute—stick to it.
- Watch the social chatting on telephone calls; it adds up; talk business first.
- Set a specific time for social chatting.

Action Item: Get real. We are our own worst enemy here.

> *"You become what you practice the most."*
> *Richard Carlson*

What might be some other common time robbers with which you have to deal?

How might you manage these?

For Fun: Ten Easy Acts to Slow it Down a Bit

1. Have breakfast out once a week, by yourself. Read the paper, plan a vacation, daydream write some thank you cards, break the rollercoaster pattern.

2. Buy a cheap vase and keep flowers in it regularly. Yes, guys, it softens the edge in the office or at home. People will comment and you might even engage in some human dialogue rather than workplace fencing.

3. One thank you card a week, handwritten. For good reason or, for no good reason such as "reflecting on what a good friend/coach/role model/sense of humor/spirit of helpfulness, etc."

4. Find an aromatic candle that doesn't make you sneeze and light it periodically while you work. You don't have to believe all the aromatherapy stuff—just do it. Be fire safe.

5. As a friend to borrow their favorite playlist and then listen to it no matter what. It will change the conversation.

6. Go shopping...for a local elementary school classroom (crayons, pencils, drawing paper), homeless shelter (soap, shampoo, razors, socks), animal shelter, food pantry...you get the picture. Get your mind off "you" for a while and feel good doing it.

7. Discipline yourself to check email / voice mail every two hours. Trust me, if it's earth shattering, someone will find you (yes, even after hours).

8. Turn off the cell phone for at least breakfast, lunch and dinner.

9. Cook something for someone 3-4 times a month. Mince, chop, marinate; unwrap the frozen pizza or cookie dough and bake. For goodness sake get

a counter top grill and do some chicken. People will appreciate your effort and I guarantee no one will complain about the food.

10. Of course, the old standbys—lift a finger: exercise, walk the dog (yours or your neighbors) stretch, take a bath (sure guys, even for ten minutes), meditate, pray, do yoga, read a book.

Might you be a "workaholic?"
Take this assessment on: www.workaholics-anonymous.org

Reflecting on Your Use of Time

Over the past few decades work life has become pretty all consuming. New technologies like email and smart phones have made it difficult for professionals to truly step away from their work lives – so much so that during the recent government sequestration (mandated cuts in government spending), many agencies of the federal government required their employees to leave their Blackberries at the office from Thursday close-of-business to Monday morning so that Congress would see a reduction in productivity that matched the reduction in funding!

As these technologies have made us so much more "productive," they have also made us much less "reflective." Yet recent research has pointed to the importance of introspection and reflection on the part of leaders and managers. It seems that successful people carve out time to just reflect on what is happening. Those who do not carve out this time get immersed in ongoing patterns of behavior that may not be serving their own interests or those of their employers very well.

Reflective time is important enough to justify setting aside some amount of time every week – whether it's one hour or one day. Over time, the return of investment (ROI) on this time will likely be very high. This reflective time offers the opportunity for new ideas and new thinking that can be turned into successful initiatives, quality improvements, or efficiency gains. In fact, successful people throughout history have found new insights by going off on their own to do some deep thinking. This is not "wasted time" – it is an investment in the ability to see opportunities that are not visible when you are stuck in the daily grind.

How might you start doing more reflective thinking right away?

"You've got to think about the big things while you're doing the small things, so that all the small things go in the right direction."

Alvin Toffler

CHAPTER 5

Successful Personal Team Collaboration

Follow-up on Self-Assessment from Chapter 1

1. What did you learn or get clarified from talking with your manager?

2. What do you need to do to maintain this level of clarity?

3. How do you plan to act upon the feedback to ensure success at work?

4. Was this easy or difficult?

Twenty Team Behaviors of an Engaged Workforce

Unless you are a bench scientist in a sequestered laboratory you have team members with whom you must interact. While everyone talks about "teamwork" very few people define exactly what is expected. We asked over 1,000 managers and staff in different work settings from the operating room to the furniture shop to tell us what teamwork looked like. Here's what they told us.

1. Completes work on time.
2. Shares information other team members need to be successful.
3. Approaches problems objectively using information and good problem solving skills.
4. Offers solutions and options rather than focusing on griping or criticism.
5. Works with the ideas of others to find effective and efficient answers and strategies.
6. Takes personal initiative for working out problems with other team members.
7. Frequently checks team agreement and commonality of focus.
8. Openly receives, clarifies and respects the comments of others.
9. Stays focused on relevant issues and problems.
10. Stays cool despite different personalities and problems of other team members.
11. Supports other team members during difficult times.
12. Encourages, respects and supports the ideas of others in team discussions.
13. Gives positive reinforcement to team members as appropriate.
14. Seeks out the feedback of other team members.
15. Asks for assistance, clarification or information when in need.
16. Models appropriate interpersonal relations in dealing with others outside the team.
17. Supports team decisions and contributes to successful implementation.
18. Willing to take on a variety of responsibilities within the team.
19. Advocates for system changes to improve work and customer service.
20. Takes personal responsibility for improvement in work, team and customer competencies.

Upon which of these would your work group benefit the most from improving?
Which of these are your strengths?
How might you help the team improve teamwork?

Supporting Collaborative Decision Making

Personal perspectives that contribute to team collaboration in decision-making

Clarity: Keep Overall Outcomes Clearly in Focus by Asking Questions

- What exactly are we seeking as an outcome?
- What problem are we trying to solve?
- What's going to happen to our ideas?

Problem-Minded vs. Solution-Minded. Fully explore the problem before beginning to look for solutions:

- A problem is a "gap" between a goal and our current state.
- Do we have a common understanding of the problem?
- Have we examined it thoroughly enough we know exactly what we're solving?
- Do we have all the data needed to scope the problem or opportunity?

Appreciative Inquiry: "Everybody has a piece of the truth."

- Seek first to understand, not to respond.
- Inquire with appreciation of the ideas of others, to learn more.
- Use open ended questions to engage broader conversation and ideas.
- For example:…"could you please tell me more, give me an example?"

Avoid Potholes to Collaboration
(adapted from The Magic of Dialogue, Daniel Yankelovich)

1. Avoid being locked into a box by anyone, including yourself.
   - There are multiple options to most challenges not just your ideas.
   - Be open to taking a look around before jumping to conclusions.

2. Avoid starting at different points.
   - Work to assure we're all solving the same problem not different ones.
   - Clearly agree on what a good outcome would look like.
3. Avoid contrarianism.
   - Different ideas are helpful; pestering, grumpy criticism is not.
4. Avoid having a pet preoccupation.
   - This is not about just you.
   - Collaboration means accommodation and compromise.
5. Avoid opera singing.
   - Ok, we heard you the first two times; cut the chorus.

Applying "Customer Relations" Approaches to Team Members and Customers

Three overall dimensions of customer service behavior apply both to customers but also to relations with your team members and other collaborators or connections outside your team. Keep these in mind as you relate to those others.

Communicate with Courtesy
- Respond quickly to people. Smile, greet warmly, introduce yourself if necessary and remember to say please and thank you.

- Maintain eye contact; also be aware of tone of voice. By all means use standard telephone or email courtesy.

- Maintain an appropriate image with dress and grooming. Maintain a clean and tidy work environment.

- Overall be seen as **helpful, gracious and personable!**

Provide Information and Rationale
- Gather information privately and protect dignity.

- Listen carefully to fully understand needs, fears, concerns and information needs.

- Anticipate information needs and offer to help. Reassure, clarify and followup promptly.

- Explain procedures and provide rationale (background on the "why").

- Give ample notice of what's to come.

- Clarify your expectations if appropriate and check the expectations of others: what have they been told?

- Make sure any printed information you're using such as instructions or guidelines are clear and easily understood.

- Take detailed messages and leave detailed messages.

- Overall, be seen as **a source of needed information and reassurance. Reduce uncertainty!**

Respond to Individualized Needs
- Reassure, be supportive and display empathy.

- Provide detailed rationale and explanations.

- Help identify additional resources for assistance.

- Don't give people the "run around:" provide specific information, handle issues yourself if possible and be courteous no matter the emotion of the other party.

- Manage conflict by controlling your own behavior and keeping your cool.

- Use active listening skills: paraphrase, take appropriate notes, empathize, attend to non-verbal cues.

- Alert other personnel to special needs, interests or concerns that you notice.

- Assist the team with special responses to challenging and difficult issues.

- Overall, **meet and exceed expectations for "helpfulness" both internally and externally.**

Sharing Leadership Responsibility

"If you're looking to get noticed, appreciated, and perhaps even promoted, look for opportunities to contribute to the success of the people around you."

Steve Ventura

Shared leadership refers to the contributions all team members are expected to make to assure meetings, problem solving and collaboration work smoothly.

Even though a manager or other team leader may be in charge of facilitating a meeting or problem solving session, it doesn't mean team members can't also contribute to leadership.

Leadership direction for effective teamwork and problem solving is needed in both the *task dimension* and the *interpersonal dimension* of the effort.

Everyone has capability in some aspect of group leadership.

Look closely at the roles below to find your strength and where you might add even greater leadership contribution to deliberations in your team environment.

Task Leadership Roles (any team member may contribute):

- Initiating.

- Clarifying and elaborating.

- Information exchange.

- Consensus taking.

- Summarizing.

Interpersonal Leadership Roles (any team member can contribute):

- Balancing participation.

- Encouraging.

- Harmonizing.

- Consensus taking.

- Appreciating.

Task Leadership Roles any Team Member Can Contribute

Initiating: Activities that focus on getting the group started, keeping progress moving, and keeping discussion focused on the problem and topic.

Examples of initiating behavior:

"Are we getting off track?"
"Do we have a clear definition of the problem?"
"What is our objective?"
"Can we clearly state our expected outcome?"

Clarifying and Elaborating: Assisting group understanding and focus by adding needed information or examples. Contributions that help everyone better understand perspective, details and implications.

Examples of clarifying and elaborating behavior:

"I'm not sure I understand. Could you give me an example?"
"Do you mean _____?" "Are you saying_____"?
"Is this a good example of what we're trying to get at?"
"I don't understand why this is important?"
"Can you share the data or evidence that you used to come up with your suggestion?"
"What information are we ignoring in our process that may be helpful to look into?"

Information Exchange: Communication behavior that assists the group in uncovering and sharing information and valuable perspective.

Examples of information exchange:

"Does anyone know anything more about this issue?"
"Here's some information I got from the accounting team."
"What do you think about that idea? (seeking opinion)
"Here's a concern I have about that idea." (giving opinion)

Summarizing: Communication behavior that synthesizes, reviews, or clarifies what has been discussed or decided; and what might be left to accomplish.

Examples of summarizing behavior:

"I'm feeling a little lost. Could we summarize where we are?"
"Here's where I think we are so far."
"Let's review what we've decided."
"Is this where we ought to go from here?"

Which of these contributions would your co-workers say you are the best at helping with in meetings?

What might you contribute more of in meetings?

Interpersonal Leadership Roles any Team Member Can Contribute

Balancing Participation: Helping people participate and distribute opportunity fairly.

Examples of balancing participation behavior:

"Jennifer, what ideas do you have?"
"Joe, why don't we let Mary finish before we hear from you."
"Robert we've heard a lot from you. I also want to hear from some of the others."

Encouraging/Appreciative: Reinforces the participation and ideas of others and encourages involvement.

Examples of encouraging behavior:

Eye contact and attentive listening behavior.

"John, that sounds like a good idea."
"I think Margaret had a good point earlier."
"Charlie, I understand what you mean, and it's a point we'll have to consider."
"Emerson that's interesting, please tell us more."

Harmonizing: Relieving tension and reducing friction within the group.

Examples of harmonizing behavior:

- Appropriate humor.
- Stepping in to point out similarities between opposing ideas.
- Suggesting compromise when differences appear unresolvable.
- Respecting the ideas of all members through polite and courteous communication.

Consensus Taking: Assisting the group to focus on closure and choice-making.

Examples of consensus behavior:

"It feels like most of us believe this idea is probably the best."
"What do the rest of you feel we ought to do?"
"Is there anyway we can combine these suggestions."
"It looks like we have narrowed it to two options. Should we vote?"
"Could we take another fifteen minutes to wrap this up before we break?"

Which of these contributions would your co-workers say you are the best at helping with in meetings?

What's common about most of these communication behaviors?

Discovering How to Add Greater Value to Collaboration

Personal success at collaboration requires learning how to be more valuable. Consider the following behaviors as a means of adding even greater value to your workplace.

Become a time and problem solving advantage for the team.

- Anticipate your manager's and team's need for information, ideas.
- Asking how else you can help the team.
- Helping customers / other staff use the manager's or team's time wisely.
- Be a great networker.
- Volunteer for critical problem solving or process improvement groups.
- Help new team members get up to speed.

> *How might you add these to your contributions?*
> *Do you know a team member who adds value here?*
> *Describe how they help.*
> *Have you told them? Why not?*

Influencing customers or other teams with whom you interact

- Clarify for others how to best interact / transact with your manager and team.
- Help outsiders do their homework about your team and processes.
- Be a source of information / broker information to others.
- Seek feedback from outside the team.

> *How might you add these to your contributions?*
> *Do you know a team member who adds value here?*
> *Describe how they help.*
> *Have you told them? Why not?*

Personal credibility keeps you a valuable collaborative leader
- Capable / dependable.
- Organized.
- Fair.
- Service oriented and easy to work with.
- Viewed as a source of "navigation;" how to manage the business maze.

> *Do you know a team member who adds value here?*
> *Describe how they help.*
> *Have you told them? Why not?*

Handling sticky communication challenges with all parties.
- Clarify expectations of others without being bossy.
- Conflict: What's the cause? How can you help? Keep it civil.
- It's all about relationships: are your communication skills helping?

> *Do you know a team member who adds value here? Describe how*
> *they help.*
> *Can you model their behavior?*

Regarding Teamwork and Collaboration

One of the skills discussed in this book that is likely to become even more important in the years to come is collaboration. There are three reasons:

- *First, technology has made most of us accessible most of the time, which means that someone working on a project can easily solicit help from others at times when in the past they would have had to figure out the problem on their own.*

- *Second, the youngest generation currently in the workforce – called the Millennials (born 1981-2000) – seem to rely a great deal on collaborative working styles. This is important since in 2018 this group will make up more than 40% of the workforce.*

- *Third, many of the challenges we currently face in our work lives and in society reach across the "silos" into which people have traditionally been organized. Decision-making processes consistently engage a broader set of "stakeholders" than would have been involved even a decade ago. As a result, it is increasingly important to collaborate across these stakeholder groups, which may speak different jargon or have vastly different points of view.*

In summary, the people in the workforce, the work we are doing, and the way we are working all call for a higher level of collaboration than was required in the past.

Reflecting on Your Team Contributions

Today's job expects you to attend to your job tasks, serve internal and external customers <u>and</u> collaborate with your team to plan, coordinate work and solve problems. If you feel like pitching in and helping out is just giving extra then you are missing the point and an opportunity to demonstrate contribution. Teamwork is part of our job expectations not something we offer when we feel like it.

Take some time and think about how your team interacts? How you work with individuals? How you meet and work as a team? What you manager struggles with in team meetings (e.g. getting participation and ideas, dealing with difficult people, achieving clarity)?

Glance back over this chapter and find one or two behaviors you might be able to try out in these team settings. Anticipate the next team meeting and look for an opportunity to apply what you've focused on. Remember, you don't have to dominate the conversation to add value. Small behaviors can contribute mightily to helping the team and advancing your own credibility. Start with something easy. Don't take on the bully right away—unless you think you're ready. Ease into your new team behaviors and soon you will find them easy and natural.

CHAPTER 6

Personal Influence

"If you want your boss to approve your idea, you have to sell them on it.
Nobody is going to focus on a dull recitation of turgid mush."

Paul Lovett

Accepting Influence

All members of an organization or team must accept certain responsibilities
in order to enhance personal influence. Consider the actions below as you take
the opportunity to influence the continual success of your organization.

Maintaining Perspective

Stay informed. Accept responsibility to use the many channels of communication providing information to staff. You can help your "success awareness"
here.

If you want information--ask for it! Management cannot read your mind and
frequently overlook providing key information we need or would find helpful.
Ask your manager about information and issues that concern you (Department
goals and objectives, new programs, changes, problems, policies).

Be alert for opportunities to participate in decision making. Department meetings, committees, and staff projects all require your input. Look for those opportunities to share your ideas. If you have suggestions, let your supervisor know. Don't wait to be asked.

Deal in solutions, not criticism. Your creative input is what will make the organization a better place. Expressing criticism and identifying problems are only one-half of the equation. Your solutions and suggestions are required as the other half. No one likes a whiner but everyone likes an idea person.

Prioritize your efforts. Not all of your concerns, problems or ideas can be addressed at once. The organization must focus its resources on the most important problems and programs first. Be realistic. Identify your most important concerns first. Better yet, focus on the key issues that concern your manager!

What information do you need you're not getting? How might you get it?

What critical challenges face your department where management might be interested in your "solution" ideas?

What ideas do you have that might assist the department?
Do you speak up in meetings?

Have you shared your ideas with your immediate manager or team leader?

Personal Influence: Offering Suggestions and Dealing in Solutions

The success of any idea or suggestion is related to the extent to which it can be seen as having an important impact.

Listed below are a few ideas for explaining the impact of your ideas. Be prepared to relate your ideas to answers to the following questions:

How does your idea impact the quality of work or services being delivered?

- Quality issues require consideration of "external" and "internal customer" expectations as well as commonly accepted professional standards.

- What do your customers want? [internal and external]

- What are the key quality issues in your area?

How does your idea relate to our efforts to reduce costs, increase productivity or produce revenue?

- Will it save money? How?

- Will it help us make money? How?

- Will it increase productivity/efficiency? How?

How does your idea impact "people" concerns? (e.g., a pleasant and productive working environment)

- Safety.
- Collaboration.
- Cross-functional communication.

- Employee engagement.
- Pleasant work environment.
- Partnership.

How does your idea relate to the goals and priorities of the department and your area of responsibility?

Does your idea impact other areas of operation?

- Will it help or hurt other areas of operation? How?

Is there a way your idea might be pilot tested first to determine its potential?

- A pilot test is a limited "test drive" of a new idea or process.

Worksheet: "Six Questions for Making the Business Case"

1. **How does your idea impact the quality of tasks or services being delivered?**

- "External customer" expectations.

- "Internal customer" expectations.

- Impact the key quality issues in your area.

2. How does your idea relate to our efforts to contain costs and increase productivity?

- Save money.

- Increase revenue.

- Efficiency.

3. How does your idea impact "people" concerns?
(e.g., a pleasant, safe and productive working environment)

- Will it make things easier for staff?

- Safer.

4. How does your idea relate to the goals and priorities of the department and your area of responsibility?

5. Does your idea impact other areas of operation?

6. Is there a way your idea might be pilot tested first to determine its potential?

Strategies for Lateral and Upward Influence

Meet your expectations. Greater credibility and, therefore, the potential for greater upward and lateral influence, increase dramatically with a solid work record. Quality, timeliness, teamwork, and customer focus all matter here. If your work is mediocre or not meeting targets, you are less likely to get anyone's attention for your ideas. If you're not a team player or known to bad mouth the the customers, or worse yet, higher ups or co-workers in the organization, you're also failing to meet the relationship standards of a quality work environment.

Know your manager's priorities. We listen most carefully when the topic concerns us deeply. We all look for helpful ideas to handle performance pressures, stubborn challenges, and personal goals with which we're dealing. The better you know your manager's pressure points the more you can link your new ideas to them as helpful choices. The more you respect your co-workers' issues the more influence you will have. If you want to get my attention, talk to me about helping me achieve my objectives, solve key problems or improve productivity!

Deal in positive solutions not negative criticism. Nobody likes a whiner. Constant criticism and a focus on what's not working turn people off. Think instead of becoming a solution partner with your team or manager by offering new ideas and options. Does the manager, or your team for that matter, hate to see you coming down the hall because they know your critical style will be abrasive? Such behavior closes doors to upward influence. You don't always have to agree with the manager or co-worker, but when you disagree it's your responsibility to offer other ideas and think them through. Try saying "yes, and…" rather than, "yes, but…."

Make the business case. Connect the dots for the higher ups. How does your idea relate directly to greater success in our business results, our customer focus and employee engagement? Do your homework here so that the value of your idea is highlighted by focusing on the outcomes to be achieved. Don't expect your audience to see the flash of brilliance you see without a little nourishing. This may require clarifying a few assumptions or working through numbers and data to sanity check your idea. The more you can do this the greater the possibility of influence.

Have a plan. New strategies and creative solutions to business challenges all come with implementation baggage. Don't let someone hallucinate about how hard your idea will be to implement. Suggest a high level plan you believe is achievable. Influence requires doing your homework. Being ready to discuss how you see implementation demonstrates you care, have done your background work, and want to be a player.

Pilot Testing. When others appear to lean toward your idea but are cautious about whether it will really work or can be easily implemented, offer a test drive option? Is there a way we can try part of your idea? Roll it out in a limited or more controlled environment? Have one team try it on for size? Managers love pilot testing because it's low risk, risk taking. If early indications don't look good they can always pull the plug on the test and minimize their risk. Always be thinking of ways your ideas can be tested with reduced risk to the organization and you'll increase your influence effectiveness.

Lob rather than fastball your pitches. "I disagree!" "That won't work." "We tried that two years ago." These responses, while possibly accurate, don't help cooperation. To gain influence you need to gain attention (connect the dots) and demonstrate your ability to work collaboratively to investigate options. Badmouthing someone else's ideas or demonstrating debating skill can turn others off. Look for common ground to build on and then offer your ideas as helpful solutions, tossed up gently to be explored rather than batted down. Use phrases such as: "Here are some options I've been thinking about." "What do you think of this approach?" "Could this be another alternative?"

Adapt to your manager's communication style. Action oriented? Likes to sleep on an idea? Prefers it in writing, email, oral briefing? Has a set of questions they ask? These managerial characteristics are important in determining your influence strategy. The reflective manager may need a small dose of your idea, sleep on it, then be ready to engage in more detailed discussion. An action-oriented manager wants you to get to the point. How will it improve our results? Be easy to implement? The manager preferring it in writing will expect it to be well thought out, organized, and comprehensive. The manager preferring the oral briefing will set the tone for the conversation and ask questions when they feel like it, requiring you to be very well prepared and agile.

Build and use coalitions. Groups of like-minded folks, using good diplomacy and working the data to make a business case, are more likely to gain attention to their idea. This is not about a band of aggressive employees pushing an idea. It is about a team of positive minded people collaborating to offer new ideas, options and quality solutions to business challenges. This is not an underground effort. It is a means to build a critical mass of support, get more wisdom working on the ideas, and polish your thoughts as the group matures the ideas.

When "NO" is the answer. Even the most credible and well thought out influence attempts will hit the wall on occasion. If you've followed the tips above it's likely you scored some points. "A mind stretched, never resumes its original form." Try to objectively understand what didn't connect. Or, understand that even with good ideas, there is only so much organizational capacity and resources and some ideas will be priorities while other perfectly good ones will wait. Your credibility has most likely been enhanced as you were seen as a pro-active solution partner.

Which of these are most likely to help you have greater influence?

The "Executive Briefings" Communication Model: Written or Oral

The "executive briefing" is a one page tool that condenses recommendations and background context for focused and efficient consideration by managers and executives. Consider the elements of an effective executive summary identified below.

An effective executive summary is 1 page outlined in 4 segments:

Recommendation: Cut to the chase with a bottom line statement of what you recommend. Or, what the dilemma/problem is.

- The recommendation, or...
- The current status, or...
- The seriousness of the dilemma.

Context: Then work backward to scope a "brief" context: anticipate the key issues of interest to the person you're briefing or to whom you are making a proposal. Scope an opportunity statement to clearly articulate the business focus. Summarize the elements in the environment, customer or end user interests, threats/opportunities, that has led to your recommendation. This might include a statement of what might happen should your recommended action not take place

- High-level evidence or data. Historical perspective/actions, survey data, positions of other key players (departments, competitors, other work teams.). High level not decimal points!
- Possibly an "acuity" rating: emergency, urgent, important, strategic (longer range).
- Strategic or operational implications (Does it tie to our operational or strategic plan?).
- Problem solved / advantage gained by the recommendation / action.

- Political implications / legal implications.
- Key point of your deliberation/research/benchmarks.
- Reasons for optimism.
- Historical relevance (any precedents, predecessor data of relevance?).

Resource implications: financial, staffing, volunteer effort, partnerships, etc. There are financial implications to all ideas!

FAQs (frequently asked questions)
- What might be the frequently asked questions?
- You've anticipated some above with your "context points."
- Timing, prioritization, other priorities that might have to be shifted?
- Think ahead to what might be asked: include a couple in your briefing.
- Be prepared to speak to the details of implementation if appropriate.

Working with Your Manager: Rules of the road

- Managers may be competent or incompetent, but they are your boss. Tread carefully.

- Managers have pressures and expectations to meet from their managers. Try to determine what those key performance expectations are and be helpful to them.

- Do not assume. Check with your manager on a regular basis to clarify work performance expectations. Be certain of top priorities, authority levels and expected timelines. This is your best insurance for success.

- Communicate with your manager using his / her preferred communication style: brief oral reports; written reports; email; formal / informal appointments; match the style.

- Protect your manager's time. Bring only the important. Be prepared. Get to the point!

- Deal in solutions not complaints. Do your homework. You'll look good.

- Never surprise your manager. Even good surprises make some people nervous.

- Don't over-react to pressure situations and conflicts; keep your cool and be a good model in difficult situations. Remember your emotions will create a response and drive the outcome. You can control emotions and thereby the response.

- Work well with all members of the organization; collaborate, pitch in when appropriate, be seen as helpful. Don't let personalities get in the way of getting the job done. Managers love the team player.

- Admit mistakes. Deal with problems honestly. Honesty will get it over and you can get on.

- Know your strengths and limitations and identify an ongoing self-improvement plan whether your manager requires it or not. If you need go get other help, get it.
  It's your career.

- Resist the temptation to gossip and talk about the manager or others behind their backs. This always finds its way back and you look like a creep whether you deserve it or not.

Managerial Characteristics that Might Offer an Opportunity to Provide Added Value

Unless we're self-employed we all have a boss. They come in all types each with their own gifts and challenges. See if you can find behaviors of your manager in the lists below. Each behavior provides an opportunity to help your manager be more successful and therefore be seen as a "value added" employee rather than just an average Joe or Josephine.

Identifying characteristics of a manager's behavior you may have known:

Absentminded	Overcommits
Impatient	Overcome by email
Too patient	Doesn't like email
Too many meetings	Open door policy
Files by piles	Clean desk fetish
Detail freak	Big chunk thinker
Micro-Manager	Likes their routine
Always in the office	Late for meetings
Always out of the office	Social butterfly
Edgy	Needs to be in control
Softy	Needs to be liked
Delegator	AM person
Hogs information	PM person
Hot temper	Moody or grumpy

Others:

No matter how frustrating these behaviors and characteristics, there are actions you can take to adapt to your manager's style and add even greater value. How might you behave with a manager who acts like this in order to neutralize your stress and possibly gain some credibility?

Managing Your Manager: Self-Assessment

My manager and I meet at least twice a year to discuss long-term departmental plans and my specific performance objectives.

What do you need to do here?

My manager is aware of all of my ideas for changing and improving our department even if some can't be implemented.

What ideas should you offer now?

When I take problems to my manager, I'm always prepared to recommend solutions.

What adjustments do you need to make in your criticisms / suggestions?

I have made my manager aware of the type of information about the business that I need in order to better do my job.

What do you need to ask about here?

I am aware of areas where my performance could be improved and have identified a plan of action to improve. I have asked my manager for assistance with self-appraisal.

What do you need to do here?

I alert my manager to work problems or pressures before they become major.

Anything on the horizon here?

71

I update my manager on major projects or tasks without being asked.

What do you need to do here?

I contribute to our business "team" effort by displaying open and cooperative communication with all persons connected to our business.

What do you need to work on here?

I am consistently mindful of appropriate public relations when dealing with persons who do business with us.

Any improvement you need to make here?

My manager and I frequently identify projects or tasks that I am able to accomplish independently or with minimal supervision.

Have you asked?

This is your career we're talking about here--give yourself an advantage by taking charge!

Successful Personal Influence and Collaboration:
Review and Key Points

"People will forget what you said.
People will forget what you did.
But people will never forget how you made them feel."

Bonnie Jean Wasmund

What team behaviors demonstrate your collaborative capability?

- Supporting the contributions of others?
- Maintaining good working relationships among team members?
- Showing appreciation and value for collaborative team members?
- Review the team behaviors on the earlier pages and choose to step up.

"Shared leadership" behaviors help teams achieve more.

- Problem solving leadership roles
- Interpersonal relations leadership roles
- What shared leadership roles do you want to be known for?

A manager's style and preferences require us to adapt in order to add value to the team.

- In what way have you adapted in order to add value?
- What else might be an opportunity to add value and be seen as a success contributor?

73

The success of your ideas and influence is related to how well you identify their potential impact on a successful workplace.

- Can you be counted on to continually look for improvement ideas?
- When you bring ideas to the manager or team, are you making the business case?

Reflecting on Influence

One component of how many people define success is having more power over others. However, it may be that influence is more important. But what's the difference?

When you have power, people have to do as you say. In some cases they may avoid you because they don't want to do what they think you are going to tell them to do. Or they may keep things from you because of the reaction they think you will have.

When you have influence, however, people seek your advice to help them make better decisions than they could make on their own. They are grateful when you give them your input. They are more confident in their own decisions and they know they are learning by collaborating with the experts. While we may think that power is the key to getting things done, influence is so much more powerful.

A three-star Army general with whom we've worked told us that over his entire career in the military he only gave someone a direct order a handful of times. In the vast majority of situations, he exercised his leadership by engaging the more junior person in an exploration of potential actions that could be taken, and then through influence directed the junior person toward the action he thought was best, or together they identified a different action that would be more appro-priate. If influence can be more important than power in a structured environment like the military – where chains of command are very well defined – then how true this must be in your organization as well!

CHAPTER 7

Interpersonal Success with Co-workers

Personal and Professional Credibility

There is one certainty of work life:
The greater your personal credibility,
the greater your likelihood of success.

To a co-worker, your personal credibility is important because it helps create confidence in our work effort and reduces tension in working collaboratively with one another.

To a manager, performance of assigned tasks and interpersonal skills are measures of a person's contribution to the organization and the degree to which additional opportunity should be granted.

In assessing personal and professional credibility, managers and co-workers generally focus on three elements of employee behavior:

1. Expertise or competence.

2. Believability or trustworthiness.

3. Personableness.

What do you believe managers and co-workers look for in each of these areas:
Expertise / Competence?

Believability / Trustworthiness?

Personableness?

>*"We must overcome the notion that we must be regular . . .*
>*it robs you of the chance to be extraordinary and leads you to the mediocre."*

The Basis of Personal and Professional Credibility

1. **Competence**. *"Expertise"* or *"competence"* refers to other people's perceptions that you know what you're doing.

While this certainly means how you're doing in specific task performance and knowledge, it involves other factors as well. Organized people, who are good problem solvers, who work well in groups, and who are good communicators, are perceived as more competent than those with fewer skills in these areas.

Therefore, while task performance is central and critical to work success, interpersonal skills are also important determinants of competence.

2. **Trustworthiness**. *"Believability"* or *"trustworthiness"* refers to people's perceptions of your character--that you are honest and dependable.

For example, people who are truthful, who do what they say they will do, and who are fair-minded have greater credibility than people who display fewer of these traits. While you may be competent in your job, you must also be trustworthy.

Competent but unreliable employees do not have credibility and therefore are customarily given less freedom and opportunity in the workplace and not counted on by their co-workers.

3. **Personableness**. *"Personableness,"* refers to the ease with which people are able to work with you.

For example, people who are good listeners, even tempered, cooperative, and appreciative of the contributions of others are considered personable.

It is not possible to be quite personable while lacking in one of the other two categories and maintain any degree of credibility over the long run. Most people can see through interpersonal "fluff" quickly, especially in the workplace where well-rounded performance is important.

To enhance career development and work satisfaction, review the more detailed outline of the factors of personal and professional credibility on the next three pages.

- *Pay attention to your strengths and where you need to consider making changes.*

- *Realize that others are watching your behavior all the time.*

- *Improvement and consistency are important in developing and maintaining your credibility.*

- *Also, be honest in assessing your strengths and needs.*

- *Successful careers are built upon the firm foundation of mature self-evaluation and commitment to improve.*

The Basis of Personal and Professional Credibility

1. Competence / Expertise

- Achieves quality work outcomes in a timely manner.
- Knows the job, stays knowledgeable.
- Prepared, always does homework/research; attends to detail.
- Adept problem solver, consistently produces results.
- Manages a well organized work area; organized, helps organize others.
- Balances multiple demands, prioritizes, doesn't over commit.
- Identifies additional resources to assist problems (people/information).
- Concise and precise in communication.
- Helps lead discussions; summarizes, focuses, leads logical progress.

Where would your manager believe you are most competent?

What advice would an honest best friend give you about where you need to improve?

What elements of competence or expertise might you work on this next year to increase your personal credibility?

2. Believability / Trustworthiness

- Follows up, follows through, keeps word, accountable.
- Withholds judgment until all information is in.

- Compromises as appropriate.
- Accepts responsibility for "opinions" on sensitive issues.
- Shares information widely.
- Admits mistakes and errors, apologizes when appropriate.
- Considered "fair" with others; doesn't "play politics" behind closed doors.
- Good listener; consistent communication style.
- Respects diversity of opinion, encourages "hearing" other opinions.
- Objectively discusses pros and cons of issues to assist problem solving.

What would your manager believe are your strongest areas of trustworthiness?

What advice would an honest best friend give you about where you need to improve?

What elements of trustworthiness might you work on this next year to increase your personal credibility?

3. Personableness / Dynamism

- Works comfortably with diversity of opinion.
- Works comfortably with differences in personal style of co-workers.
- Works comfortably across different ethnic and cultural groups.
- Available, approachable, cooperative.
- Shares knowledge and information easily.
- Maintains even disposition, sense of humor, laughs at him/herself.
- Respects team expectations: collaborates, respectful, supportive.
- Doesn't bad mouth others.

- Good listener, involves others, solicits input from quieter people.
- Assertive but not aggressive, speaks confidently within/before groups.
- Suggests rather than criticizes, compliments others, sincere praise.

Where would your manager believe you are the most personable?

What advice would an honest best friend give you about where you need to improve?

What elements of personableness might you work on this next year to increase your personal credibility?

Enhancing Credibility through Effective Listening

Good and respectful listeners are usually perceived as more credible!

Facts: About 40-50% of a professional's workday will consist of listening.

Most people listen at about 30% effectiveness. Of 100% of our potential to accurately attend to someone's communication we effectively use about 1/3.

Poor Listening: The three most frequent causes of poor listening include:

- Faking attention but thinking about something else or multi-tasking, texting or emailing.

- Reacting emotionally to someone personally, or his/her ideas, rather than hearing them out before evaluating and reacting.

- Rehearsing your answer while someone is still speaking.

Negative Listening: Many of listen with more of a "parent" or judgmental ear rather than a "peer" or supportive ear. Listening to make judgments may distract you from the core information, emotion or facts. Seek first to understand. Be careful.

Effective Listening: Good communicators aren't perfect. They actively focus their skills.

- Objectively **evaluate our own biases and skills** and focus on becoming a better listener.

- **Take notes** on even the shortest conversations. This will help you focus.

- **Don't interrupt others**. Be patient. For lengthy comments it may be appropriate to interrupt to clarify or gently remind the speaker that you have only limited time.

- **Withhold evaluation.** Listen completely before deciding your position.

- **Don't mentally rehearse** your response while you're listening.

- **Don't hide confusion or uncertainty**. Often your lack of understanding is the speaker's fault for lack of clarity. Gently ask for clarification.

- **Clarify meaning and assumptions by paraphrasing** what you heard the other person say. The paraphrase is introduced by the phrases "Do you mean...?" or, "Are you saying...?"

- **Ask for specific** examples to help you better understand what someone else is trying to communicate. This will increase clarity and reduce speaker exaggeration.

- **Review frequently** during long task or business conversations so that you keep on track. You keep the speaker focused and you both enhance understanding. Refer to your notes.

- **Assist the "rambling speaker" by gentle interruptions** to clarify and get examples of what they are talking about, or a succinct statement of what they want.

- **Don't overreact** to emotion laden words or criticisms. Keep your cool and hear the other person out, listening carefully for the underlying emotions.

- **Summarize** conclusions, actions, and agreements orally before finishing.

Benefits of Improved Listening: Improved problem solving effectiveness. Fewer mistakes. Enhanced personal credibility.

Fundamentals of Effective Communication at Work

Clear and concise. That's the standard for effective communication in today's workplace. Clarity comes from understanding the purpose of your communication and zeroing in on that purpose right away. Concise comes from not telling your life's story but summarizing enough information that the listener—your boss, teammate, friend—can decide how much more they need or want.

Use the following tips as a checklist for making your communication more powerful at work.

Understanding your purpose:

- In a busy professional environment you have about one minute to get someone to listen to you and clarify what you need. After that, you lose their interest.

Are you clear what you need from this communication exchange?

- Advice; support; clarification; action; "heads up?"

- Possibly begin with a statement of purpose.

Have you made your needs clear to the listener?

- "What's your reaction to this?"
- "What do you think of this?"
- "What would you do here?"

- "I need your help / support."   "Could you give me a hand by...?"

- "I want to make sure this is clear."
- "I want to check to make sure I understand."

85

- "Here's the outcome needed": What action? When? Meeting what standard?

- Get to the point!
- Take a good look at the executive summary model on earlier pages as a template.

Providing rationale:
- Here's why I'm concerned; need this; need this done this way.
- Here's how it relates to: you, our department, customer, quality, costs, employees.

Being Specific:
- Here's an example of: what I saw; what it should look like.
- Be specific. People remember specific examples and facts.
- Be specific with examples without being emotional.

Fundamentals of Effective Communication at Work

Be Diplomatic:

- Pleasant and supportive language and tone of voice convey collaborative rather than hostile intent.

- When you make a mistake in tone or appropriateness, take a breath and apologize.

- Everybody likes to feel they have input into things happening around them: are you inviting input? Effectively listening? Encouraging other points of view?

- You can welcome the suggestions and ideas of others even though you may disagree.

Courteous Yet Direct with Difference of Opinion

- "I just see it differently."

- "I understand why you feel that way."

- "That's not an important issue for me."

- "Complaining is not helpful. Do you have a suggestion?"

Adapting to the Receiver:

- We all listen with our experiences and biases as a filter; use words, phrases and examples that I will understand.

- Styles: some people are action oriented while others are analytical: be patient with both.

- Some people are more excitable while others take communication events in stride: stay focused on how and what you are communicating regardless of reaction.

> **Fifty percent of the time communication goes awry it's the <u>fault</u> <u>of the</u> <u>sender</u>.**

Effective Communication for Accepting Assignments that Work

Clarity drives success because you cannot be successful without clear expectations. In the workplace this applies directly to your job assignments, outcomes expected and any other assignments you might be given.

Consider the following actions and behaviors as you go about assuring "clarity" for your work expectations:

- Are there clear written objectives that spell out the parameters (boundaries) of your assignment as well as the outcomes expected? If not, make notes as you're receiving the direction.

- Do you feel you're capable of delivering? If not, have a conversation about your concerns or how to get the assistance you feel you might need to deliver.

- Are there resources, training, access to information or people you believe you will need?

- Clarify the "authority" level you may have to complete the assignment or task.

- Can you see clearly how this task / assignment is related to the departmental and organizational goals and objectives? Ask enough questions to be clear on this.

- Are there clearly defined progress dates and deadlines for accomplishment or delivery?

- What feedback does your team leader or manager want along the way? Scheduled updates? Important milestones? New wrinkles you've discovered?

Can you adequately summarize your assignment and all the "clarity" issues identified in this guidance to someone else if you had to? That's the test of clarity!

The more complex and higher risk the assignment feels, the more important it may be to go back to the person giving you the assignment and summarize your understanding of the elements listed here as a means of checking clarity before you start.

Finally, deliver ahead of schedule if at all possible!

Working with Virtual Teams

Today's workplace may find you in a more "virtual" setting than a traditional work setting. Eighty-five percent of U.S. workers find themselves collaborating on projects with colleagues in other offices. The challenges of engagement, communication and managing stress can all be exacerbated by distance.

Fruitful relationships with colleagues and managers don't happen by chance in a more virtual setting where face-to-face relationships are now supplanted by internet, groupware, and email. While we know positive feelings about communication and other workers increases when we work face-to-face, we also know that connectedness and sometimes identity can be challenged the more isolated we feel.

Making sure you have clarity on job deliverables and that what you're working on is aligned with what the boss wants can be more challenging when there is distance between you. Personal accountability must replace management oversight to some degree so virtual success depends even more greatly on you being focused and a disciplined self-starter. Engagement is harder to demon-strate when telephones or email are our forms of communication but none-the-less the behaviors of highly engaged workers from our earlier chapter are still relevant.

Here are some thoughts on remaining "visible" even when you're not in the building.

- When you do have face-time with co-workers or your boss make it count. Be very prepared and know what you need and they need when you meet.

- Help your "virtual" team build some rules of engagement—how do you expect one another to behave on conference calls, email protocol, pushing information and updates, etc.

- If you haven't heard from a significant team member or your boss for some time pick up the phone and connect. Lack of communica-tion can cause gaps in everyone's confidence—don't let that happen between you and others. E-mail is not as effective here.

- Make sure you have a written work plan that you review quarterly with your boss.

- Be assertive about an "electronic of telephonic" open door with your boss—retreating away when you need assistance or clarification does not help your success.

- Use the "task and interpersonal" leadership guides from our earlier chapter on conference calls. People need facilitation, encouragement and your clarification to also be effective contributors even on confer-ence calls.

- Don't fall victim of the rumor mill—if you hear about something that you're curious about or upsets you, check in with your boss.

These Phrases Kill Successful Collaboration and Reduce Your Personal Credibility.

- Not my job!

- Everybody else does it!

- That will never work!

- We've tried that before!

- We've always done it that way!

- It doesn't matter!

- It's good enough!

- Someone else will do it!

- Not my problem!

- I don't care what other people think!

- I don't need any help!

- I just do what I'm told!

- They don't pay me enough to do that!

- Some rules were meant to be broken!

- I just put in my time and then get out of here!

What are people usually thinking when they blurt out these phrases?

If we're feeling this way, what might be a more credible way to express that thought or feeling?

If a co-worker says this to you, what's a reasonable response?

Interpersonal Success with Co-Workers:

Review and Key Points

"Search others for their virtue, and yourself for your vices."
R. Buckminster Fuller

The greater your personal credibility the greater your likelihood of success.

- *What do you need to do to demonstrate even greater credibility?*

    To your work team?

    To your manager?

- *What would an honest friend tell you about your "real" credibility?*

Effective listening and clear sending of messages helps teams be more successful.

- *What one thing do you need to work on to be a better listener?*

- *How can you make your communication even clearer and more credible?*

Differences of opinion and difficult people are a part of the workplace. They require each of us to monitor and manage our own "reactions."

Reflecting on Communication

Communication is as much about what your body conveys as it is about what comes out of your mouth. We communicate non-verbally through our eyes, facial expressions, and body positions. To test this, try having the same conversation with a colleague from the following two positions:

> *Position #1: Sit in a chair with your legs shoulder width apart on the floor in front of you, hands at your sides, and head looking straight at your colleague.*

> *Position #2: Turn your body to the left by 45 degrees, cross your right leg over your left, cross your arms, and turn your head to look at your colleague.*

What did you notice? Did the two positions feel different from one another? Ask your colleague about his or her experience during the two conversations.

Many people who do this exercise report feeling much more open to their colleague and much more able to listen attentively while sitting in the first position. In the second position, they feel closed off from their colleague. You can think of the space between the front of your body and the front of your colleague's body as a "channel" of non-verbal communication. Anything that blocks that channel – e.g., your arms, legs, or even a table or desk – prevents some of that non-verbal communication from taking place. You are likely to feel more closed off and less able to be present with the person to whom you are ostensibly listening.

In some conversations, keeping that channel open may be difficult. If it's a contentious conversation or a deeply personal conversation, the experience of the non-verbal communication across that channel may be too intense. That's OK. The key is to be aware of what is happening in that channel – whether you are opening it or closing it. If you find that you consistently fold your arms, cross your legs, or obstruct the channel in any other way, see if you can return to the first seated position described above, where you are fully open to your counterpart. Or if you have difficulty keeping the channel open with a particular person, give some thought to whether or not there is an emotional dynamic between the two of you that is making you feel threatened and unable to listen fully. If there is, then that would be a great thing to communicate about!

CHAPTER 8

Tension and Stress
When it Gets Stressful

"They say it's better to be poor and happy than rich and miserable.
Wouldn't it be better still to be moderately
wealthy and just a little moody?"

Unknown

Every workplace has its share of stress.

When both work and home challenges are pressing, stress can make us feel less energetic and more afraid. Stress also impacts our ability to maintain good relationships at work and home and get quality work accomplished.

- *What are some typical sources of stress at work?*

- *What are some typical coping mechanisms you or others use to deal with the stress?*

What are the most pressing sources of tension and stress for you?

- At work?

- At home?

Target them for change, no matter how small, as you read this chapter!

Think about the small changes you can make right away to reduce tension and stress?

- Set some goals and act promptly: goals without action don't get accomplished.
- The more intense the stress the more you should ask friends or professionals for help.

Are you investing your time wisely to maximize personal success?

- Priorities at work?
- Managing priorities at home.
- Work from a plan to assure focus and assertiveness with time investments.

Coping with Tension and Stress in Our Lives

"No matter how badly you act, no matter how unfairly others treat you, no matter how crummy the conditions you live under are...

...you virtually always have the ability and the power to change your intense feelings of anxiety, despair, and hostility."
Albert Ellis, How to Stubbornly Refuse to Make Yourself Miserable About Anything, Yes, Anything

Most of us simply wish we could change our reactions to events rather than making a conscious decision to change our reactions.

Since much of what is defined as stressful is determined by our individual perceptions of what we are reacting to as a threat or opportunity, the greatest determinant of how we manage stress is how we perceive it.

Let's take a look at some typical coping styles and understand how to more positively change our outlook.

Some on-line resources on stress you might find helpful:

- **Resource: on-line stress test: http://www.lessons4living.com/stress_test.htm**

- **A popular "Rational Emotive Behavior Therapy" worksheet to analyze your stress target actions to reduce your negative perceptions of what's happening: www.stressgroup.com**

Typical Stress Coping Styles

Victim Syndrome
"Oh poor me, I've been taken advantage of again."

Many people perceive of themselves as victims, suffering without control over life's events, subjected to the whims and fancies of others without recourse.

The *"Oh poor me, I've been taken advantage of again" reaction* is a popular and unsuccessful coping mechanism yet it frequently gains us sympathetic attention from peers.

This unhealthy self-talk is a dangerous means of trying to resist stress because it **fails to face up to our own capability and capacity to gain control** over our life situations.

Unhealthy Self-Talk:

"Why can't I catch a break?"

Application reflection:
Think of a co-worker or friend that has demonstrated this coping style. What advice would you give them about taking charge of their stress?

Healthy Stress Management Suggestions:

- You have choices. Are you making the right ones?

- Your past experiences in successfully moving through difficult situations provides a template for success again. Think back about past success and how you made healthy choices.

- Get better informed; information is power and allows better personal planning.

- Discover options by staying in the game rather than withdrawing and whining.

- What are the things you can do without asking permission? Gain control.

- Build coalitions with others who have good coping techniques.

- See your problems as potential teachers: What's the lesson? What can you learn?

- Ask a trusted friend to give you a reality check: is your life really that bad?

- If you're really down, seek out your organization's Employee Assistance Program, a local crisis center, your personal health care provider or a psychologist.

Asking for help is a sign of strength, not weakness!

Catastrophist

This is also known as the "Past and Future Anxiety Syndrome." Many people spend much of the time thinking about (worrying about) the future disasters and catastrophes that might befall us or reminding ourselves (and often regretting) disasters of the past.

Not only does this mental anxiety eat up positive energy and increase our tension, it also prevents us from developing a **"present awareness"** necessary for gaining control of the here and now. **Fix, don't blame!**

Remember your Álgebra. E + R = O. "E" is your emotions, and when added to your reaction "R" the outcome "O" is determined.

Change your thinking and change your life.

Unhealthy Self-talk:

"But I see so much that could go wrong."
"I've lost trust and confidence and know it will get worse."

Application reflection:
Think of a co-worker or friend who has demonstrated this coping style.
What advice would you give them about taking charge of their stress?

99

Healthy Stress Management Suggestions: "If it's predictable it's preventable."

- What can you do right now? Focus on getting the present in a good grip. Adjust today.

- What did you do before that resulted in success? Focus on building on these lessons.

- What are the real odds of death defying occurrences happening?

- Been caught by "surprise" before? What have you learned about being better prepared?

- Back up plans are smart investments if you seriously anticipate some turbulence ahead.

- Envision future events that make you anxious by seeing them ending positively rather than starting at a negative outcome.

- If you've lost trust, it's not unhealthy to be tentative. It's best to talk openly about this.

Can't or Won't Say No

This is also known as the "Complacent Paradox Syndrome." Our lack of assertiveness, and the inability to say no, allows our gates to stay open for additional stressors.

How often do we find ourselves in commitments because we were not man or woman enough to say "no thank you, not this time," or we fail to recognize that having priorities and standing by them is O.K.!

You must say "no" to some choices in order to make your "yes" more valuable.

Those of us who feel we must please everybody and fail to speak our piece cope with the stress it produces by feeling we are "irreplaceable" or "don't want to hurt someone's feelings."

Unhealthy Self-talk:

"I didn't want to do this in the first place, but I kept quiet."
"Well, if you think this is what we should do..."

Application reflection:
- *Think of a co-worker or friend that has demonstrated this coping style.*
- *What advice would you give them about taking charge of their stress?*

Healthy Stress Management Suggestions:

- If hesitant, listen to that voice and say, "let me think about it."

- If certain, be assertive with your "no's".

- If you feel a wrong course is being taken, speak up and ask others, "Does anyone else feel a bit tentative about this?"

- If you've said yes and started a journey, volunteer assignment or project that you now feel you should have said no to, ask for someone's help in revisiting it and possibly getting out.

Can't Catch a Break

This is also known as "My Lot in Life Syndrome." In the movies, at the next table in the restaurant, that co-worker over there, they all seem to have the good life. Everybody is happier than me and it must be my lot in life to not have access to the opportunities others have. I can't seem to catch a break.

"I've had bad luck!"
"I get hit so hard because I can take it and others can't. I need to carry the ball."
"I don't have the tools, capacity, intelligence, good looks, and money to break out of this life!"

"I'm a woman and must passively accept this!"
"I'm a man and must carry this burden; be tough."

Unhealthy Self-talk:

"Gosh, I must not be deserving."
"Why does everybody else get the breaks?"
"I'm strong, committed, and a 'go to' person. I'll push harder."

Application reflection:
Think of a co-worker or friend that has demonstrated this coping style.
What advice would you give them about taking charge of their stress?

Healthy Stress Management Suggestions:

- If you are alive, you have stress in your life

- If you have a job, you have stress in your life.

- If you have a family, you have stress in your life.

- Do a plus and minus list of "things to be thankful for" and "stresses / strains of life."

- What tools /skills / coaches / mentors do you need to create more opportunity?

- Who can you talk to who can provide a "sanity" check? Someone who will tell you if you're just whining or not?

Perhaps it's your poor choices that have contributed to where you are rather than luck or pre-determination.

How can you invest more time into activities that help you appreciate life? (e.g., family, spirituality, education, sports, travel, gardening, fishing)

When It Really Gets Stressful

Success at managing tension at work may benefit from gaining control in four distinct areas:

✪ Perception Control: *seeing the stress in a different light.*

✪ Environmental Control: *changing surroundings to modify tension.*

✪ Relaxation Control: *using breaks and "time outs" to recharge.*

✪ Physical Control: *healthy physical choices reduce tension.*

Perception Control: "Choose other interpretations"

- Recognize your "choices" in reacting to events: *we choose to be angry, frightened, hostile, embarrassed.*

- No one <u>makes</u> <u>us</u> "react" a certain way. *Don't take the bait from the grouch or the hothead.* Take control of your emotions and reactions and thereby the outcomes.

- Establish / confirm priorities; this changes the importance of many current stressors. You'll find some things are not as important as you thought they might be.

- Are you really indispensable? Can others help out? Try asking.

- Psyche yourself up:

  - Anticipate tough situations (high volume, challenging situations, timelines, interpersonal relations) and mentally rehearse your choices, actions and successful outcomes.

- Anticipate needed tools, information, and planning. Get a handle on them.

- See yourself in control. Recognize your strengths and how they will be put to good use in upcoming situations; others will be happy you're there and helping.

- Pat yourself on the back. You've managed difficulty before and survived.

- Analyze some of your lesser stressors by measuring them in minutes compared to days and weeks; they jump into perspective as minor irritations rather than major battles.

- Reconsider needed states of perfection; we are not perfect, but we can be more aware:

  - Your family doesn't need a perfect dad and mom they need a sensitive dad and mom.

  - Admit your limitations and don't try to push them; work around them.

  - Identify your developmental needs (skills, education, counseling) and address them.

Environmental Control: "Change Your Environment. Get Organized!"

- Change your environment, spatial arrangements, brighten work and home environment. Change your routine.

- Work from a plan: objectives /pathways/ timelines and stick with it. Recognize short-term accomplishments.

- Reduce your overload. Cut back on some things to substitute relaxation time or fun agenda items.

- Not everything pressing down on us must be done at the current pace or on the current schedule. Adjust pace and timing now.

- Give something up; say no to new commitments; De-clutter NOW.

- Schedule stress reduction time in your plan: make an appointment with yourself to exercise, take a break/day off, close the door and be alone, seek out the company of friends.

- Contract with yourself, your family, and your boss for targeted priorities and stick to your plan.

Reflection

Over the course of our careers, hopefully we gain awareness of how and where we do our best work. Some people really do their best work the night before a project is due. Some people really need to break it down into steps that can be spread out over time. Some people need a neat and clean work environment that is organized with a file for each project or task. For other people, putting something away in a file turns into "out of sight, out of mind," and important balls get dropped.

You might want to look at the photo of Albert Einstein's office on the day he died—very messy [see the photo at: imgur.com]. Obviously his preferred working environment was a little more chaotic than many of us would like. But he was successful in that environment, and it could be argued that he might not have been as successful in a more organized office with nothing left out on the desktop. What was important for Einstein is that his environment supported the way he did his best work.

How do you do your best work? Do you work best in bursts of creativity that move you significantly toward your goal in a very short period of time, or do you work steadily over a longer period of time? Do you work best outside in the fresh air or in an enclosed space where you are isolated from potential distractions? Do you need your workspace to be neat and orderly, or would you have felt quite at home in Einstein's office.

Write down some of the key attributes of the places, practices, and processes that have helped you do your best work in the past. Now, for each attribute you wrote down, brainstorm how you might increase the extent to which those attributes are reflected in your current work situation.

- *Can any of these opportunities be adopted immediately?*
- *Will you need to negotiate some with your boss?*
- *Or is your current working situation far enough from what tends to make you successful that it is worth considering an even larger change, like getting a new job altogether?*

A great deal of success is finding the situation where you are apt to be successful, so be intentional about creating the type of environment you need to do your best work.

Relaxation Control: "Take Ten Minute Vacations"

- Relaxation response: take a few deep breaths, stretch, get some fresh air, change your scenery, take a time out just for yourself.

- Possibly a walk around the building will be more relaxing than joining other conversations at break time

- Visualization/meditation: focus on mental images of a tension free environment, spiritual images, a favorite relaxing space; keep a favorite photo that makes you smile close by.

- Talk out your stress with a willing and empathetic listener; a counselor if you're really tense about something.

Reflection

Many people tell themselves that they do not have time to relax, to meditate, to exercise, etc. They are just too busy. But as Buddhist teacher Tara Brach says, "You can take one breath." Even the busiest person in the world has time to take one breath each day from a place of relaxation and reflection.

To do this, sit up comfortably in your chair with your feet firmly on the floor, shoulder width apart. As you inhale, imagine that you are breathing in cool, refreshing energy from the world around you. Hold the breath for a few seconds to let it go all throughout your body. Then as you exhale imagine that you are breathing out all the stress and tension that is in your body. Let the out-breath relax you completely.

You may find that the first breath feels so good that you want to do another. And another. You may decide to make this a regular practice in your life, maybe even a few times a day. Having some kind of relaxation practice like this can be hugely beneficial for pulling you out of the stresses of the moment and allowing you to get a broader perspective on what is going on and what you can do to improve the situation. And remember, if you tend to fall asleep when you do a practice like this, it does not mean that you are doing it wrong. It just means you need more sleep!

Physical Control: "A ten minute stroll is beneficial to mind and body."

- Good nutrition, balanced diet and caloric intake. A little improvement helps.

- Exercise/physical activity: divert emotional tension; build physical capacity.

- Even short walks are beneficial.

- Careful with alcohol consumption—this is not a medication!

- Do you have any hobbies you can plan more of?

- Possibly take 10 minute intervals of flurried effort to tidy, clean, organize, etc.

Reflection

Many behaviors, such as eating sweets, drinking alcohol, or gambling, can become addictions. Many people have addictions without knowing it. In essence, an addiction is something we do to avoid a situation that we consider intolerable. Addictions help us avoid having to deal with some underlying emotion that we have in that situation.

But emotions are there to tell us something. They give us information about the things happening in our lives and what they mean to us. For example, a feeling of fear tells us that we may be threatened. A feeling of anger tells us that we may have been treated unfairly. A feeling of sadness tells us that we may have been hurt, or we may have lost something important to us. In other cases, the threat, injustice, or hurt may not exist in the current situation; something may have triggered unresolved feelings we have about some situation we encountered in the past.

In either case, there is value in being with the emotion you are feeling rather than jumping into some addictive behavior in order to avoid it. (Of course, if the emotion is so strong that experiencing it fully may create an unsafe situation for yourself or others, then seek professional help in the form of a mental health care provider – e.g., a psychotherapist.) In many cases, you will find that the "dragon" – the emotion you are

111

avoiding through the addiction – becomes much less frightening as soon as you stand up to it face to face.

Make a list of the behaviors you consider as your "weaknesses," in the sense of "I have a weakness for..." Is it chocolate? Alcohol? Video games? Pornography? What do you do when the stress gets to be too much?

Write down the situations in which you are most likely to engage in the activities you just listed. What is going on in your life that makes you want to retreat to those addictive behaviors?

Stay on the lookout for those situations. When they happen next time, instead of doing the addictive behavior, sit down comfortably and take a few deep breaths. Try to name the emotion you are feeling. Ask the emotion what it is trying to tell you – what it can teach you.

Again, if you suspect that the emotion may be intense enough to create an unsafe situation for you or others, please seek professional help. Do not attempt the process described here.

Stress and Our Personal Lives: Canceling Invitations to the Stressor Family

Pick your fights wisely.
Not everything is worth arguing over. Stay out of disagreements or conflict that's not that important to you. Don't take the bait. Say "that's interesting," and walk away.

Contract with your family.
Discuss use of family time, recreation, and individual chores that help a busy family life go more smoothly. Children can and will understand and commit to contracts. And, they will hold you accountable also.

May Day, May Day.
Take stock--how bad off are we? Really? O.K., work is stressful, you're not getting the help you need at home to cope with kids, work, and having a personal life. It's going around. But exactly how bad is it? Fish don't see water and possibly we don't see some of the options, solutions or different interpretations that might help us see the world in a better light. Most of what we encounter is normal to most family and work lives. Cut yourself some slack. If things are really bad—seek some help. That's exactly what Employee Assistance Programs, your employers confidential counseling service, is there for. Experts give expert advice. Successful stress management may require expert advice.

Geek warp warning. Ask your friends, how uncool are you?
Do you feel fully strung out? Out of the ordinary orbit of life? Hostile, moody, withdrawn? Well, check with your good friends for some honest feedback and hear it as good data for your current and future success. Chances are (a) you're handling the stress better than you think (possibly not as good as you would like); and (b) you might get some helpful advice from your friends.

Modeling behavior helps others cope better and stay out of your hair.
Goodness! As scary as it seems, you are a role model for someone else about handling stress. Certainly children watch parents and other adults closely. But so do co-workers, managers, friends and other family. Making good choices demonstrates to others that it can be done and helps them see their own path.

Everyone needs a break.
The pace of 21st Century life is indeed grueling at times. More pressure, higher expectations, job security and family life dilemmas keep us on our toes. A generally busier lifestyle encroaches on time to unwind. Yet, everybody needs a

break. If we can't take care of ourselves it's more challenging to take care of work and family. Give yourself a break. Take a Monday or Friday off. Plan that relaxing weekend off, the one night a week without a hectic family schedule when you can all chill. Use your vacation for a least a bit of down time instead of all those chores piling up.

Reward positive behavior—say it out loud.
Letting other people hear our appreciation contributes to a more harmonious and collaborative work place. And it makes us feel better by activating pleasant thoughts and diverting the brain from toiling over our worries. Tell someone thanks today. Reach back and let someone know how their act of kindness, support, or helping hand cut your stress. You'll both feel better.

Hardiness, versatility, creativity, not perfection.
Sometimes we are too hard on ourselves. Stress management does not mean free from stress. Tension is common to life and work. Few of us have the perfect life, family, job, social situation or emotional balance. Make your life balance goals "reasonable" not perfection. Don't compare yourself to others who seem to have it all and lead a stress free life; most don't. Count your blessings, give yourself permission to be less than perfect and continually seek new answers and tools to reach your goals.

Work from a financial plan.
Money plays a role in about fifty percent of serious personal and family stress. Even those in reasonable financial health find "challenges" to their dreams and daily budget. This is one area where having a firm plan and maintaining some discipline with that plan will help reduce unneeded stress. Oh, we still may not have all we want but at least let's try to manage what we have prudently. Your credit union and bank have credit counselors and financial planners for even very basic needs. Get some advice.

Wellness sensitivity.
Overall physical health contributes to our capability to cope with the everyday stressors of life. This is something over which we each have individual control; we're not dependent on someone else for healthy living habits. Exercise, reasonable diet, regular health checkups and finding time to relax will pay dividends.

We all occasionally feel the sting of stress and we respond in ways that are not helpful. No one is perfect.

As long as these slip-ups are not frequent and not mean spirited, we can all benefit from showing a little more patience, cutting others and ourselves some slack, and making sure we use healthy stress management techniques.

As Will Rogers reminds us, **"Its great to be great, but even greater to be human."**

What one or two things can you do right away to chill out some of that stress?

Give it a try these next couple of weeks and see how it works.

You might consider telling someone close to you who you trust your intent—it will help with your resolve and they can become your cheerleader and supporter.

Building Personal Resiliency

Resiliency is defined as an internal personal and organizational capability to reframe life's current challenges into opportunities for growth to move forward with positive direction and renewed energy.

"Outcomes are determined by the perceptions we apply to the situation"

In both personal and work experiences how we label a situation often determines the approach to the resolution or the action needed.

- Stress within today's personal and work environment has been used as a broad label for life events, physical exhaustion and demands of time or effort.

- This broad label has become a cultural connotation that can signal negative thinking approaches.

- Blanket negative approaches result in individual and team reduced engagement, energy, and creativity.

Test your perceptions in situations. React to each statement and quickly decide if you generally perceive the statements below as a potential opportunity or as a potential threat.

- *Being asked to present before your work peers.*
- *Being asked to meet with someone in authority.*
- *Being told your role/work is being shifted to a new job.*
- *New leadership is being named for your unit.*
- *Seeing in the paper your organization is in negotiations to be merged with another.*
- *Informed of company reorganization in structure.*

Key Definition

Researchers have defined stress as an <u>individual</u> perception of an event, thought or actions that is <u>perceived</u> to have either positive or negative outcomes; either a threat or an opportunity with important personal consequences.

- *Critical to understanding stress is the concept of individual perception that determines both the outcomes and importance.*

- *Stress can be positive or negative and many times it is in how it is perceived.*

Personal Reflection

Write down two recent "stressful" events. Take a moment to consider what would have changed if you had perceived the events differently? What if you had used some of the earlier ideas in this chapter as approaches? Would the outcome have changed in the short or long run?

Personal Resiliency Approach vs. Stress Approach

The Personal Resiliency Approach builds off the positive life experiences that allow an individual or group to rally with energy, creativity and engagement to move beyond the initial perceived stress.

Resiliency is defined as an internal personal and organizational capability to reframe life's current challenges into opportunities for growth to move forward with positive direction and renewed energy.

Personal Resiliency has five steps.

- Respond.
- Reconnect.

- Reframe.
- Rebuild.
- Rebound.

RESPOND is the initial perception of the situation to be addressed. This early perception and thinking of the situation as positive or negative, threatening or not is critical. Here is where the line between panic and action is drawn.

- Critical to a successful response is to stop and pay attention to what you are feeling about the situation and its impact on you.

- Is this response appropriate for the situation?

Write down some typical responses you have seen people have to a common situation like a change in leadership at work. Notice the different responses.

RECONNECT is the moment of connecting the perceived situation to a past experience.

- Have I been in a similar situation?

- Were you able to apply successful techniques that either resolved the situation or allowed you to move through it successfully?

- How did you successfully get through it?

- What learning and capabilities can be applied? What network of support has been used in the past or is available to move forward?

Identify at least one situation where past experience(s) were able to help you begin to move through a difficult situation.

REFRAME is a process of determining what is influencing your perception of the situation.

- We frame (give meaning to) situations through self-imposed stories that we seldom question.

- These stories have been influenced by culture, attitudes, fear, assumptions and personal beliefs.

- These result in frames of reference that are often self-limiting and determined by the past.

Think through the influences that impact the stories, beliefs, attitudes and assumptions regarding life experiences? Will changing these influencers improve your ability to reframe a situation?

REBUILD is the power of resiliency. A new approach or reality is created through a conversation and self understanding of the resources applied in past similar situations and the support of others that resulted in moving successfully through an experience.

- By changing the perception of the story you create an opportunity to change the story and engage in developing a positive response.

REBOUND creates a positive vision of hope about what can be rather than an overwhelmed feeling of defeat to the situation. This in turn changes the ongoing response to the situation, how it is perceived and creates the energy for success.

Resiliency Rebound Model

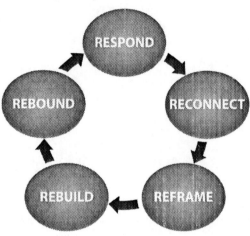

Application Exercise

Describe how you feel about a "stressful" current situation and the impacts it has on you and your work group? (physical, emotional, relational, focus and productivity at work).

Reconnect and reframe the situation around what personal intention will move you forward in a positive direction?

Using the concepts of Reframing, Rebuilding and Rebounding, what will you need to move forward in a positive direction?

Reflecting on Stress Reduction

This module has addressed your personal success from a variety of perspectives in order to give you the tools you need to think more systematically about how your attitudes and behaviors are opening or closing doors for you. Hopefully they have prompted new awareness that you can use immediately to change your interpretation of what is happening in your life – that is, your "story."

We all tell ourselves stories – interpretations of the things that have happened in our lives – to make it OK for us to have done the things we have done, or to have felt the way we have felt. We assume that the actions we take follow logically from the stories. However, in many cases the opposite is true: we make up the stories to rationalize to ourselves the actions we have already taken! This is backed up by research in neuroscience, which has found that the limbic system (the part of the nervous system most closely related to emotions) responds to a situation much more quickly than the neocortex, where cognitive thought takes place. This means that we all have a tendency to live in stories that while they help justify our past actions may in fact not be true.

Use this insight to look at some of the stories you are currently telling yourself about events taking place in your life at work or at home:

- *What is your explanation for what is happening in your life – that is, what story are you in? (The coping mechanisms listed in this module are good examples of stories that many people use.)*
- *Where has this same story played out in your past?*
- *How far back can you remember this story being a part of your life? (Many of us live in stories we created in our childhoods when our egos were not strong enough to handle the strong emotions we felt in a certain situation.)*

Now:

- *Write the story down in a few statements that capture the essence of your explanation for what is happening in your life.*
- *Now change the sentence so that it has the opposite meaning. For example, if your first statement was, "My boss does not respect people who have not come up through the ranks of our company," then change the statement to read, "My boss does respect people who have not come up through the ranks of our company."*
- *Now try to come up with evidence to support the new statement you just wrote. In this example, can you think of someone from another company that your boss does respect?*

If you can find some evidence to support the new statement you wrote (which negates your original statement), then this shows that the story you are using to justify your feelings is – to some extent – either inaccurate or incomplete. However, if you live in that story, you will only notice the evidence that supports the story. Being intentional about the stories in which you choose to live your life is a key aspect of any successful life.

CHAPTER 9

Difficult People

Working with Differences of Opinion

Some people react to the expression of different points of view and ideas as if they were personal attacks. Indeed, sometimes they are! But even when not meant to be, or even when our confidence level can handle such disagreements, we have learned that not all people are mature enough to handle differences of opinion without being defensive. Immature people tend to label every disagreement as a dent in their self-esteem.

How do skilled communicators allow for the airing out of ideas and diverse points of view while protecting the dignity and self-esteem of others? How do they press their points while minimizing hostility or alienation of others? **They constantly adapt communication style and language, and watch <u>what</u> they say! Let's take a look.**

Communication Style

- Learn to withhold judgment. Hold that quick trigger that wants to blurt out, "I disagree." Possibly say "hmmm, let me think about that."

- Ask questions to more clearly understand. Be careful of your own assumptions.

- Demonstrate good listening skills and sincere interest in getting the facts and full picture. Assure others that you understand the "whys" and "wherefores" of their position, including the data (or lack of) upon which they base their case.

- Ask open-ended questions that will lead the speaker to clarify their position.

- When you must disagree, try to find areas of commonality or agreement to emphasize. Building upon agreement, however minor, shows that you want to be cooperative rather than antagonistic.

- When disagreeing, also work to maintain a respectful tone of voice so that it matches the supportive language and style you're attempting to develop.

- Differences of opinion are healthy to a creative work environment; manage your communication style choices to make sure you're heard and not tuned out.

- Opinions or positions are influenced by the data and information we select to support our position. Ask and seek to understand what data or information you have chosen to ignore to support your position.

Less Confrontational Language

- Avoid using confrontational language. Don't make the disagreement personal.

  - Speak to the facts.
  - Focus on the problem.
  - Be hard on the problem and soft on the person.

- Instead of personalized phrases like…"You don't understand" or "You're making a mistake here."

  - Use expressions like "My experiences have been different."

  - Or…"I view that information from a different angle."

  - Or…"I'm not sure I've gotten all the facts yet. Can you give me a specific example of that problem?"

- When you must confront distinct differences of opinion, choose language that indicates your respect for the person:

  - "I can respect your perception of the issues. I see it differently and here's why."

  - Or… "I'm not comfortable yet with the same conclusions based on that information."

- Whatever you say, always give your reasons for disagreeing succinctly and without suggesting that you are smarter than anyone else.

- When you feel alternative ideas or solutions must be explored… choose language that poses your issues and concerns less confrontationally, yet gets them put on the table:

  - "What about this alternative?"

  - "Does this have a bearing on what we're looking at?"

  - "Could we look at XYZ?"

When direct confrontation is unavoidable, choose language that puts the weight on your own perception, rather than accusing the other person of being wrong.

- "Jack I'm concerned that we're overlooking the significance of idea X, and I need to get that in the record."

- "Martha, I really need you to know that I don't think this is a good idea. I'm not judging you, but want you to hear that I'm still not convinced."

- "I need your help, Bill. Let's make sure we're both not overlooking something here. Would a second look or second opinion be worth the investment?"

Communication Content

- Always be prepared to deal in suggestions and solutions.

- Make your objections and suggestions as concrete as possible.

  - Be specific and use specific examples.

  - Abstract ideas and concerns are more likely to create communication problems with difficult people.

- When you blow it, when the quick trigger or personal accusation creeps into your relationships...behave like a professional:

  - Call a time out. Admit you over reacted or got off on the wrong foot.
  - Acknowledge that you were attacking the person rather than the problem.
  - Apologize.

Reflecting on Differences of Opinion

Has anyone ever blamed you for something you didn't think was your fault?

> *How might you handle this without whining or sounding too defensive?*

A co-worker presents what you believe to be a bad idea during a meeting.

> *How might you diplomatically nudge back?*

Want to practice? Use these at home with your partner, parents or children.

Can you think of some current examples of "differences of opinion" in the workplace that would be helpful to approach differently?

Dealing with Chronically Difficult People

General Strategy

1. **Control**: Controlling your over reaction to the difficult or hostile situation contributes greatly to managing the reactions of others.

2. **Prevent**: Using effective <u>customer</u> <u>relations</u> <u>skills</u> <u>with</u> <u>everyone</u> will reduce the number of difficult people with whom you must deal.

Attention, courtesy, diplomacy and information are magic elixirs!

3. **Redirect**: With the unreasonable person your first goal is to redirect their behavior to being reasonable (emotionally in control), then to garner their cooperation, then possibly they can be moved to become satisfied with your assistance / service or cooperation.

    Redirect: Unreasonable *to...*

                     Reasonable *to...*

                        Cooperative *to...*
                        Possibly Satisfied

- Of course some people won't respond or change their core grumpiness.

- You may have to refuse to let it alter your emotional control.

- Be assertive, reasonable, and helpful but don't have a cow yourself.

Dealing with Chronically Difficult People

Strategy of Control

- The anger and frustration from the unreasonable person is frequently with the situation (conditions, policies, etc.) or their own personal issue. NOT YOU!

- You happen to be the individual upon whom they can take out their frustration with the situation: *Don't overreact!*

- If your reaction escalates to match the emotional level of the unreasonable person it will be more difficult to move back to more reasonable states of behavior. *Don't get in the ring for a fight.*

  - Once your personal reaction is out of control (emotional, raised voice, frazzled) the unreasonable person will then "personalize" their rage at you with cause: because you're acting rudely and inappropriately.

- Don't deny a person's anger or frustration. It is their reaction, whether reasonable or not. Denying their emotion will enhance defensiveness.

  - Empathy ("I can understand your frustration," or "I can see why you feel that way") allows the person to be right, even if they may be expecting too much or have misinterpreted in the first place.

- Individualize your attention to the person:

  - STOP   what you're doing to give undivided attention.
  - LOOK   directly at the person to non-verbally indicate your attention.
  - LISTEN   quietly while the person explains, vents, etc.

- If it's an uncalled for personal attack:

  - STOP   what you're doing and give undivided attention

  - BREATHE   take a second to compose yourself—don't throw gas on the fire.

  - LOOK   directly at the person to non-verbally indicate your focus

  - ASSERT   indicate your don't appreciate the attack and will appreciate them leaving you alone; walk away or look away.

Dealing with Chronically Difficult People

Strategy of Re-Direction

Relationship and perceptions change when communication changes.

Your responsive, focused, courteous communication will change many people's perceptions and behaviors.

For co-workers, customers or others who choose continued difficult behavior, you must manage the situation to maximize positive outcomes and minimize personal frustration.

People Displaying Hostile & Aggressive Behavior

Characteristics	*Tactics To Stabilize and Re-Direct*
▪ Bullies & intimidates others.	*Stay cool; speak calmly and assuredly; maintain direct eye contact.*
▪ Criticizes & argues excessively.	*Don't take it personally; agree when right.*
▪ Believes there's only one answer.	*Allow them to ventilate; empathize.*
▪ Reacts defensively when resisted.	*Allow them to save face; don't personalize.*
▪ Makes broad general accusations & claims.	*Calmly ask for specifics.*

Focus conversation on what you can do rather than what they feel you can do.

- Seize any point you can agree to and use it to move back to the issue & solutions.

- Display empathy with frustration; correct the wrong if possible or at least indicate intention to follow-up.

- Pick your fights wisely. Only disagree or confront when important.

- Apologize if appropriate.

People believing they were wronged or are frustrated

Characteristics	*Tactics To Stabilize and Re-Direct*
▪ Feels cheated out of rightful due.	*Empathize with their frustration.*
▪ Demands more than can be delivered.	*Explain constraints calmly; "So let's focus on what we can do."*
▪ Needs or wants more than is possible.	*Identify and coach to other resources; focus on what we **can** do right now!*
▪ Treated wrongly or inappropriately.	*If right, apologize and indicate intent to start correcting the situation right then.*
	Empathize; display immediate focus of attention on the subject person.
	Clarify: these are the limits of my authority, time, knowledge, etc.
▪ Chronic complainer.	*What do you think we should do? Get to suggestions.*

People who become emotionally distraught / cry

Characteristics	Tactics to Stabilize and Re-Direct
▪ Lost control; overwhelmed; can't cope.	Empathy; emphasize positive options; "You have options"; "Let's get started turning this around right now!"
▪ Won't stop sobbing.	Call a time out; "Take a moment and then we can get started." Physically leave or get up for some moments; Emphasize that options are open.

Don't show frustration; speak in a calm, soothing voice; slow physical movements; break eye contact; provide for privacy to reduce embarrassment. |

Staller / Wet Blanket / Uncooperative Behaviors

Characteristics	*Tactics To Stabilize and Re-Direct*
■ Beats around the bush; hints.	*"I need your help"; "I can help if you will be specific."*
■ Needs lots of positive reinforcement.	*Reinforce positive behavior as well as good decisions; express confidence in their ability to decide.*
■ Won't be specific; "You know...."	*"Give me a specific example"; "Let's start from the beginning"; explain you can't go on until they provide more detail...then be quiet.*
■ Won't agree until everything looks perfect.	*Indicate importance of making commitment and getting started; break solutions into segments / phases and suggest they re-evaluate at milestones.*
■ Won't work; not confident; tried before.	*Don't argue; express confidence; find a sliver of agreement / confidence and focus on it.*

Dealing with Difficult People in a High Pressure Environment

Some additional perspectives on issues, perceptions and team relationships of working in a busy environment

- **The Team**: Supportive, helpful, and understanding relationships within the work team will prevent stress and enhance positive focus.

    Stress statements from co-workers:

    - "I'm working harder than anybody!"

    - "It's not my fault. I don't make these decisions!"

    - "Get off of my case."

    - "If they had done it right in the first place."

    - "What do you mean you couldn't find it; it's right here bozo!"

    - "Don't bother me now. Can't you see I'm the busiest one here."

Which of these co-worker stress behaviors are most difficult to deal with?

What strategies / responses might be most effective?

- **Co-Worker and Customer Issues**:

    Situations of unreasonable co-workers:

    - Lost: *forever lost in the wilderness; always behind, flummoxed and clueless.*

- Big Cheese Syndrome: *all attention on me and me alone; nothing's right!*

- Quick is NOT Quick Enough: *I need it done right now!*

- People who feel we should all be like Mother Theresa: *Why aren't you perfect?*

- Average Joe and Josephine never appreciative of success: They say: "So what. I expected things to go smoothly."

Which of these co-worker stress behaviors are most difficult to deal with?

What strategies / responses might be most effective?

Working with Differences of Opinion Worksheet

Recall a disagreement you've had with another employee or manager.

Describe the circumstance and how it ended:

What went right?

What went wrong?

When there is conflict or disagreement in your work life, what is it typically about?

What have you read here so far that you might use next time a difference of opinion surfaces?

Bully Proofing the Workplace

Workplace bullying is a global problem. International studies as well as U.S. studies show that bullying in workplaces, much like school bullying, occurs in just about every type of workplace. Workplace bullying can impact millions of people each day. The stress caused by bullying impacts not just workers but their families.

When bullying occurs the most vulnerable are often the youngest, least experience workers and on the opposite scale sometimes the oldest *("Hey old man! Getting too old for this job"?).*

Women, people of color, different ethnic backgrounds or sexual preferences are most often those targeted. Anyone who is different and not likely to retaliate or complain may become a bullying target. Bullying is built around a desire to control or exert superiority over another person or group.

Test your workplace bullying climate:

1 = Strongly Disagree   5 = Strongly Agree

1. Co-workers don't always treat each other with respect.
   1   2   3   4   5

2. New employees have to prove themselves through tolerating teasing before being accepted.
   1   2   3   4   5

3. Differences in people (lifestyle, age, gender, preferences) are being talked about by one or more employee

   1   2   3   4   5

4. We have had workers who left because they "just didn't fit in" not because they couldn't perform.

   1   2   3   4   5

5. Someone is always on the "hot seat" for something not work related.

   1   2   3   4   5

6. Differences are embraced in our work team as to what makes someone unique.

   1   2   3   4   5

7. We have very specific "cliques" among workers.

   1   2   3   4   5

8. People swear a lot as part of their work and conversations.

   1   2   3   4   5

9. Some of my workers are considered threatening in their voice or actions

   1   2   3   4   5

10. Status, seniority is very important in my workgroup.

    1   2   3   4   5

If you answered a four or higher for any question, it reflects a likely bullying situations in your workplace. If your over all score is 20 or less your workplace is likely bully proof. 21-30 indicates a need for further investigation. 31+ indicates behaviors that are considered bullying are occurring.

Reflection / Application

Think of a time when you felt bullied or saw someone else bullied?

What could you have done, said or acted on that might have stopped the bullying?

Typical Bullying Behaviors: Check those you have seen or experienced.

- Hitting or touching without permission.
- Invading personal or workspace uninvited.
- Spitting.
- Damaging or hiding personal property.
- Swearing.
- Yelling
- Name calling.
- Verbal put downs.
- Excluding/isolating from the group.
- Verbal threats.
- Butt of jokes.
- Racial slurs.
- Sexual slurs.
- Workplace fights, violence.
- Humiliation.
- Offensive Texting/Emails/ Social Media posts.
- Mean looking stares as a response.

Reflection / Application

Think of a time when you were the person who was bullied (you may have to go back to elementary school). What feelings did you experience about yourself, your capabilities, and your future?

Think of a time when someone stopped a bully. How did you feel? Was there a sense of relief, safety, and celebration?

Cyber Bullying the New Trend

Social media such as Facebook, Twitter, My Space together with emails, texting and various video and photo share sites have become outlets for bullying in the workplace. Workplace computers, email, and smart phones used to bully other workers have resulted in employee terminations, lawsuits and workplace violence. So, be very cautious with how your electronic communication can be perceived.

Six Simple Social Media Rules Regarding Bullying

- *Use employer furnished equipment only for purposes related to your work.*

- *Remember that everything connected to media, the internet, and communications is discoverable and can and will be used against you if someone feels wronged.*

- *Always write, speak, text, send information as if it was going to be viewed by everyone or published on the front page of your local newspaper.*

- *Remember mom's rule # 1: If you can't say something nice, don't say anything at all.*

- *Negative labels or descriptions of people that are not substantiated facts should be avoided.*

- *Personal social media should be treated as carefully as work tools. When you post something about your boss or employer thinking it only is going to be seen by your friends, remember you don't control whom they forward it to or where they post it.*

Caution: many employers are now requiring to access and review an applicant's "Facebook" account prior to offering an job. Will yours support the credibility you are looking to portray?

Keys to a Bully Proof Workplace

- Bullying thrives in a climate of silence and fear. Supervisors and team leaders need to create an atmosphere of openness to speak up about unwanted behaviors linked to bullying. Talking about bullying behavior in the workplace will start to break its hold as an acceptable behavior.

- Set an example of mutual respect in both words and deeds. Words can hurt even when implied in a teasing manner. If someone doesn't feel comfortable empower them to speak up and ask that the uncomfortable words or behaviors cease immediately.

- Developing a zero tolerance for bullying in the workplace will help to eradicate it, especially if clear procedures and consequences are spelled out. Report instances to your human resources office.

- Empower yourself and co-workers in the stand up, speak up rule. Individuals need to stand up against bullying in the workplace too. Co-workers need to support each other by standing up.

- Take bullying reports seriously, and encourage they be investigated thoroughly and suggest calling in external consultants if necessary to ensure impartiality. Interventions need to be followed up to ensure that behavior changes result.

- Demonstrate a positive communications environment that excludes use of derogatory terms, innuendo, implied threats, and duplicitous statements. Positive communication and work environments reflect respect for the strengths of all team members.

Reflecting on Working with Difficult People

- *How might you adjust your communication response to the challenging situations and people bringing conflict and tension to your life?*

  At work?

  At home?

  If it's your immediate manager?

- *What's the most important thing you can do to reduce the tension associated with working with difficult people?*

- *How well do some of these "response" tactics work in your home environment?*

- *What might you try?*

CHAPTER 10

Driving Your Own Career

Career Planning

You have goals for your work career. It may be you're quite happy with what you're doing or it may be you have exceptional stretch goals for where you would like to be. We know that goals without plans seldom are accomplished. We also know we can to some degree create a higher return on any opportunity that might present itself if you have in mind where you want to go and end up in your work life.

As you anticipate planning a career please take a moment to reflect on the following questions:

- What are you passionate or excited about? What do you really like doing?
- Can you see yourself doing that work? For a lifetime? Are there some elements of that work you might not find attractive?
- What might be the benefits and limitations of the work you have an interest in?
- Where do you find those jobs? Within your current employment? Elsewhere? Are you willing to relocate?
- Are there salary implications important to you? Can you meet those and be happy with this new work?

- What are the educational requirements for those jobs? Do you have it? Are you willing to go get it?
- Do you see yourself in a management leadership position in this career some day? Have you scoped out what that might imply? Have you talked to anyone in management or leadership to see how they see the requirements and challenges of that level of career?
- What does your family think of this career objective? What might worry them? How might they support you?
- What actions, commitments, assistance might you target over the next year or two to move closer to achieving this career objective?

Driving your career through Networking and Social Media

"Sometimes, idealistic people are put off by the whole business of networking as something tainted by flattery and the pursuit of selfish advantage. But virtue in obscurity is rewarded only in Heaven. To succeed in this world you have to be known to people."

U.S. Supreme Court Justice, Sonia Sotomayor

Understanding Networking

- Networking is about setting up and maintaining relationships that can help you professionally and personally.
- Networking is about being connected to or knowing the right person, vendor, supplier or employee at the right time to help a situation.
- Networking is critical to individual success both within and outside an organization.
- Most people do not consider the importance of networking until they find themselves seeking a new position.
- Despite the growth of web based job boards and electronic posting of resumes, the most successful job hunter realizes that it was networking that got them the job.
- The broader you network and maintain network health within your place of employment the greater the likelihood of promotions, increases in pay and responsibility.
- There are some basics to networking that are critical to being seen as trustworthy and successful.

"The person who is knowledgeable about how they are perceived by others is twice as smart as someone who only views themselves through their own eyes"

Assess your networking status

- I have a LinkedIn free account with a profile that has been updated within the last 3 months.
  Update LinkedIn regularly by:
  - Posting positive activities, accomplishments.
  - Recommending others.
  - Suggesting articles, books, blogs related to your profession.
  - Participate in LinkedIn discussion / interest groups.
- I attend trade meetings, conferences, company sponsored events where I can meet other people.
- I use Twitter, Facebook or other social media as a way of praising colleagues; informing people of my organization's or my success.
- I respond to emails in a positive and fast manner that are succinct in content with direct subject line headings.
- I respond to calls from recruiters with offers to help them find someone even if I am not right for the job.
- I respond to inquiries from colleagues and network members with offers to share my connections.
- I regularly stay in touch with my network through calls, emails, tweets, face to face meetings.
- I look at trade meetings, conferences and company events as not a business card trading frenzy, but a chance to get to know someone and for them to get to know me.
- I've posted a professional summary on "About Me" [about.me]

Reflection

Where are there opportunities to improve your networking?
What three things can you do in the next 30 days to improve your networking?

Guidelines for Successful Networking

- **Consider how you want others to see you** and know your reputation. You have the power to build an online profile that you like, but make sure it matches your reputation off line.
- **How you treat people is and will be a part of your story.** Following the suggested behaviors in the earlier chapters will distinguish you from others in a very positive light.
- **Networking is a quid quo pro relationship.** Positioning yourself as a good listener, a connector to others to help them expand their network will create a willingness of the part of others to assist you when you seek a contact or information.
- **Look for a positive networking opportunity** at every meeting, conference, and interaction with another person.
- If your company doesn't provide you **business cards** have some personal ones made up with your contact information.
- **Practice your opening networking conversation.** Have a brief 20-30 second statement of who you are and what you do and an engaging positive question that shows your desire to learn more about others.

"You don't know who knows whom that can be critical to enhancing your career"

Real life Lesson: Dennis Remembers

I remember being at a training session of a large employer when I introduced myself to a young man who looked lost in the group. A colleague said, "that's just some new intern, ignore them and they go away!" I introduced myself and sure enough he was a new intern working one of the lowest customer service roles. We had a nice conversation where I encouraged him to feel free to reach out to me anytime for coffee or lunch and I would be as helpful as I could in his adjustment. The next day I received a call from the President of the Board of Directors, thanking me for being so nice to his nephew. I indicated I had no idea who his nephew was, I was just being welcoming. From that day on, as he shared his story with other board members and executives, I found a new level of appreciation for my role as a manager at the company. You just don't know. Again, you mother was right when she said "be nice to everybody, you never know who they know!"

Reflection

Where have you had a positive result of meeting some-one (networking) that played out in your career?
Think about your level of comfort in speaking with strangers or people you perceive as more successful, smarter, powerful than yourself. What skills do you need to work on to gain greater comfort in networking with these individuals?

Leveraging Social Media

What do you need to do to improve your networking and social media presence?

- Linked In
- Facebook
- Twitter
- About.me
- Web
- Personal business cards

Reflection

What do you know about how others perceive you as a person, employee or in other roles?

List networking opportunities for face-to-face meetings and introductions that could enhance your profile and reputation.

Ask others to introduce you around.

The Don'ts of Networking

- Don't be negative about your employer, job, co workers.
- Don't use social media as a place to complain.
- Don't forget to say thank you and show appreciation to others.
- Don't forget that the internet doesn't discriminate between business and personal life. It is always there now and forever.
- Don't push. Build relationships over time and based on common interests.
- Don't engage in discussions or jokes that you wouldn't want published in your name on the front page of the morning newspaper.

CHAPTER 11

Putting It All Together

"You can only fail if you give up on something."

Jonas Salk

The world is now changing so quickly that many of the old ways of doing things do not work anymore. Many of the old jobs may not even exist anymore--you may be seeing this in your organization or in your industry. Many people (maybe you) have jobs that did not exist twenty, ten, or even five years ago.

The same may be true for you as an individual. It may be that many of the ways you have done things in the past are no longer appropriate for the times or for where you are in life and what you would like to do. Every moment is an opportunity to look at ourselves to see if what we are doing is likely to take us where we want to go.

In the last ten chapters, we have presented you with many tips and tools that will help you get where you would like to go--to help you be successful. We've written about linking your work to your organization's mission, using your time more wisely, working with and influencing team members, building credibility, reducing stress, and taking ownership of your own career. We have written about the behaviors in each of these domains that will be critical to your achieving the success you've always dreamed of.

But there's a catch. Success is not something far-off that you have to work toward over many years. You can be a successful person right now. Since all of these are behaviors, you can adopt them today. Why wait? You can be a successful person today--and tomorrow, and the day after that--just by adopting more of the behaviors of successful people.

Think back to what we said at the very beginning: that we work to live, we don't live to work. That means that it is ultimately our own happiness and fulfillment in our work and in all other aspects of our lives that constitute success. What happens at work is to some extent beyond our control. No matter how good our ideas are for moving our company forward, the good people working at our competitor across town may have even better ideas. And good for them if they do! It means that they are performing at high levels, which is probably bringing them some amount of professional fulfillment. (And it's probably making our lives better by making our industry more efficient, improving the products on the market, and spurring us to perform at even higher levels than we otherwise would.)

Success is not measured externally. Success is measured in one's own terms according to one's own definition. We wrote earlier about how different people measured success. What makes something a success is that someone wanted it to happen, and they made it happen. The nature of success is in the satisfied intention it represents. Success is the fulfillment of human potential in some domain in some way that adheres to the standards of decency and integrity. It is impactful self-expression in the world.

By this point, you probably have a pretty good idea what success means to you. You've gone through the exercises in this book to take a hard look at how you go about your work, how you work with others, and how you behave in a wide range of situations. You may have determined that you need quite a bit of clarification from your boss if you are going to be successful. You may have discovered that you are really in the wrong job or career altogether. You may have identified significant biases in your own thinking that are creating patterns in the unsatisfactory results you are getting. No matter your specific situation, the purpose here is to define what success means to you, and to start acting – today – in a way that embodies that definition of success. That is what it means to be a successful person.

This is not to say that external measures of success, like increasing productivity, improved work processes, or awards and accolades, are of no value. Quite the contrary. These external measures provide hints and milestones along your own personal journey. They tell you, "it looks like you're headed in the right direction," or "there may be an interesting opportunity for you down this side road." Similarly, the setbacks you will inevitably encounter may be saying to you, "take another look at how you handled that situation," or "are you sure you are being your best self?"

But the milestones are not the journey; the external measures are not the success you're looking for. Successful people are those who achieve their dreams. They are able to do this because they believe that their dreams are valid--no questions asked. They look within themselves to see what they want out of this life--impact, significance, love, connection to a larger community--and they go about getting it. Their lives unfold with ease because they know themselves, they know their potential, and they are committed to making that potential manifest in the world. They alone determine whether or not they are successful.

And since no one else can see into the depths of their heart, they alone will know. Success by our definition requires integrity, and only you can be the final judge of whether or not you have aligned your behaviors with your vision of the type of person you want to be. Other people may assess you based on the behaviors they can see from the outside, but only you will know the real reasons why you did what you did. This is why the external measures of success are of limited value when assessing one's own life: looks can be deceiving. Before you close this book, write down the three things that you know you need to change about your attitude or behavior right now in order to be a successful person now. We know that you will probably refer back to this book, so you will likely have other insights in the future about how you could change for the better. But get down at least three things right now. Then think about what behaviors you would prefer to the ones you've been using, and identify an opportunity--hopefully within the next 24 hours--to start putting the new behaviors into practice. You will be creating new habits here, creating a new way of "showing up." So be intentional about what you would like that to look like.

We hope you have enjoyed going through this book and all the ideas and exercises it offers. We have enjoyed writing it for you. We enjoy knowing that you will take some of these ideas, put them into practice, and reap rewards in your personal and professional life for years or even decades to come. We have a profound sense of gratitude for your interest in these ideas and for your commitment to your own success.

If you are interested in bringing *Personal Success in a Team Environment* to your workplace, we are pleased to offer you a *Personal Success* "train the trainer" program that takes the trainers you choose in groups of 15 and teaches them how to use the workbook through online and classroom instruction that makes the concepts come alive. They will then be in a position to energize success throughout your workplace.

We can also provide your meetings with dynamic speakers who can address the broad or narrower aspects of personal success covered in our workbook and leave your workforce upbeat and ready to think and act differently.

Last but not least, we can provide individualized personal coaching from entry-level employees to the executive suite. Our talented and experienced coaches bring years of experience in helping people navigate their present and find their future. To find out more about these options, please contact Les Wallace at les@signatureresources.com.

In any regard, we urge you to take seriously the learning you have experienced as you have gone through this book. Define success for yourself and make it a reality in your own life. Get to it!

References of Potential Interest to the Success Journey

H. Beckwith and C. Beckwith, You, Inc.: The Art of Selling Yourself (2007).

Peter Block, The Answer to How is Yes: Acting on What Matters (2003).

Wayne Breitbarth, Power Formula for LinkedIn Success 2013).

B. Brillstein, The Little Stuff Matters Most (2004).

Richard Bolles, What Color Is Your Parachute? A Practical Manual for Job-Hunters and Career-Changers (2013).

J. Canfield and J. Switzer, The Success Principles: How to Get From Where You Are to Where You Need to Be (2004).

R. Carlson, Don't Sweat the Small Stuff (2002).

R. Carlson, You Can Be Happy No Matter What (2008).

J. Davidson, The Complete Idiot's Guide to Assertiveness (1997).

J. Dean, Making Habits, Breaking Habits: Why We Do Things, Why We Don't, and How to Make Any Change Stick (2013).

J. Ditzler, Your Best Year Yet! Ten Questions to Change Your Life Forever (2011).

A. DuBrin, Human Relations for Career and Personal Success (2014).

A. Elkin, Stress Management for Dummies (2013).

A. Ellis, Feeling Better, Getting Better, Staying Better (2001).

G. Gallagher, Stress Management: An Easy to Understand Book Full of Tips and Tricks to Fight Against Everyday Stress and Anxiety (2013).

R. Hanson, Hardwiring Happiness: The New Brain Science of Contentment, Calm, and Confidence (2013).

C. Hyatt and L. Gottlieb, When Smart People Fail (2009).

B. Kipfer, 14,000 Things to Be Happy About (2007).

H. Kushner, When Bad Things Happen to Good People (2007).

J. Maxwell, Teamwork 101: What Every Leader Needs to Know (2009).

E. McFarland and J. Saywell, If^2: 500 New Questions for the Game of Life, Vol 2 (2007).

M. McKay and P. Fanning, Self-Esteem 2000).

G. Namie and R. Namie, The Bully at Work 2009).

A. Oade, Building Influence in the Workplace (2010).

T. Rath. Strengthsfinder 2.0 (2013).

R. Roffer, Make a Name for Yourself: 8 Steps Every Woman Needs to Create a Personal Brand Strategy for Success (2000).

D. Schawbel, 4 Steps to Building Your Future (2010).

C. Smith, Difficult People: Dealing With Difficult People at Work (2013).

C. Thomson, Stress Relief Without the Bull: The No-Nonsense Stress Management Revolution of Positive Detachment (2014).

B. Tracey, D. Booher and B. Worthley, Converse with Charisma: How to Talk to Anyone and Enjoy Networking (2010).

L. Lowndes, How to Talk to Anyone: 92 Little Tricks for Big Success in Relationships (2013).

P. Murphy, Always Know What to Say—Easy Ways to Approach and Talk to Anyone (2013).

D. Zack, Networking for People Who Hate Networking: A Field Guide for Introverts, the Overwhelmed, and the Underconnected (2010).

Authors Bio-Sketches

Les Wallace, Ph.D., is the President of Signature Resources Inc. and a veteran of 30 years of work with employee success factors and high performance organizational cultures. His coaching programs for managers, leadership program for executives and work on the role of the board of directors in assuring an organizational culture where employees can excel are all recognized in the literature. Les believes everyone who chooses can be successful.

Dennis Derr, Ed.D., is a seasoned Fortune 100 health executive and consultant highly regarded for his lifelong advocacy for supportive workplaces that enable employee productivity and organizational success. His deep understanding of the behaviors that create high performance organizational cultures has been called upon by clients across the globe for over 30 years. As counselor, coach and executive, Dennis has always been the voice of the importance of employees in any corporate decision conversation.

Eric Meade, MBA, is a coach, futurist, and visioning facilitator who helps individuals and organizations define what success means for them and then take steps to achieve it. His work is consistently described as "mind-bending" and "paradigm-shifting." Eric serves on several nonprofit boards and advisory councils where he pushes for systems that more actively promote the personal success of employees. Eric believes that we all have within us everything we need to be successful.